GRACE BEFORE MEALS

RECIPES AND INSPIRATION
FOR FAMILY MEALS AND FAMILY LIFE

Father Leo E. Patalinghug

with Stella Snyder

DOUBLEDAY

New York London Toronto Sydney Auckland

DOUBLEDAY

Copyright © 2007, 2009, 2010 by Leo McWatkins Films, Inc.

Published in the United States by Doubleday Religion, an imprint of the Crown
Publishing Group, a division of Random House, Inc., New York.
www.crownpublishing.com

DOUBLEDAY and the DD colophon are registered trademarks of Random House, Inc.

Previous editions of this work were published in the United States by Leo McWatkins Films, Inc.,
in Hunt Valley, Maryland, in 2007 and 2009.

Scripture texts in this work are taken from the New American Bible with Revised New Testament
and Revised Psalms © 1991, 1986, 1970 Confraternity of Christian Doctrine, Washington, D.C.,
and are used by permission of the copyright owner. All rights reserved.

Library of Congress Cataloging-in-Publication Data is available.

ISBN 978-0-307-71721-4

Printed in the United States of America

10 9 8 7 6 5 4 3 2 1

First Doubleday Religion Edition

ACKNOWLEDGMENTS

My Heavenly Family: Father, Son, & Holy Spirit, Mother Mary, my Patrons, Saint Leo the Great, Saint Joseph, and the whole Communion of Saints (that just about covers them).

My Earthly Family: My most loving mother and father, Carlos and Fe; my supportive and loving siblings, Maria, Carlos, and Angelica; my grandparents; uncles; aunts; cousins; the best in-laws a guy could have; and the coolest and cutest nieces and nephews!

My Church Family: The former Archbishop of Baltimore, Cardinal William Keeler; his successor, Archbishop Edwin O'Brien; the parish family of St. John Catholic Church in Westminster, Maryland; my home parish of St. Rose of Lima in Baltimore; my supportive brother priests who suggested I share my passion for kitchen conversation with others: Rev. Msgr. Joseph Luca, Rev. Msgr. Arthur Valenzano, Fr. Erik Arnold, Fr. Brian Nolan, Fr. Michael DeAscanis; the faculty, staff, students, and seminarians at Mount St. Mary's University, and all of my brother priests, seminarians, and religious women and men who have shared my meals and my desire to help bring families closer to the real Banquet to come.

The Grace Before Meals Family: Tim Watkins for his daily commitment to God's work (and not to forget, for picking up the tab)! His wife, Susan, and their beautiful children; Stella Snyder, who shared her God-given talents; Shelly Mulligan for keeping the project on track; Phill Bednarik and Mike Little for their creative eye and designs; Dan (Riz) Fleuette for his skill in operations; Don Aboff for his print expertise; Chris Beutler for his enthusiasm; the Hullett Family, who opened their home to film the pilot episode of our companion TV series; and the many individuals and families who opened their kitchens and pantries to help us put the *Grace Before Meals* philosophy to the test: Jason Bloom, George Convery, Jim Decker, Laura Fick, Katrina Heiser, Kate Karbowniczek, Kathy Knapick, Liz Massanopoli, Matt McDermott, the Mohideen Family, the Mulligan Family, Tien Pasco, Nicholas and Kate Piché, Gay Pinder, Evgeniya Prokhno, Kate Reckner, Jaime and Jesse Robertson, Kathy Sirkis, Julianna Wittig, Suzanne Cannole, Teresa Hughes, Dottie Dunn, Gail Buss, Nancy Wolfinger, Margaret Fletcher, Theresa Greene, Susan Foley, Teresa D'Epagnier, Donna Walker, Myra Corbit, Sue Berger, Donna Kelly, Sue Hopkins, Sharon Beaver, Susan Lakomy, Edie Foster, Vicki Mascalco, Dawn Walsh, Billy Schroeder, the O'Donnells, Donna Brown, Rob and Robin Bosch, and Greg Hutsell.

CONTENTS

Never a Day Without Grace!

OUR MOVEMENT GROWS WORLDWIDE

When they had finished breakfast, Jesus said to Simon Peter,

"Simon, son of John, do you love me more than these?" He said to him,

"Yes, Lord, you know that I love you." He said to him, "Feed my lambs."

JOHN 21:8—10

Daniel and Deborah Slavinskas take the GBM message to heart by helping to cook an Italian meal for their son Jonathon and his classmates.

Since the first printing of *Recipes for Family Life*, not a day has gone by when I haven't received an e-mail or phone call regarding our Grace Before Meals movement. I say "our" movement because it's not my idea. It's God's idea!

And this simple concept is now catching on everywhere! I have received wonderful and encouraging feedback from readers in Australia, Japan, the Philippines, the Netherlands, Canada, South America, Nigeria, Spain, Germany, Italy, and almost every state in America. Thousands more have joined our online community at www.gracebeforemeals.com. Through our website, weekly e-mail blasts, and blog, I have not only had the chance to share some of my personal faith and culinary adventures, I've had the pleasure of learning how families from all over the world are adopting the principles of Grace Before Meals into their daily lives.

I want to stress that Grace Before Meals is truly *our* movement. It takes you and me to spread this simple but profound message of strengthening relationships around the dinner table.

Filming a cooking segment for one of our webisodes.

At first, some of my brother priests teased me about the movement being a "schtick." But, as soon as they hear the theology that supports our movement, they begin to realize that perhaps bite-sized theology is a great way to teach people about faith, hope, love, and life. There's an information overload in our world. When do we have time to discuss and digest all that's being crammed down our throats? Well, God gives each of us an almost sacred place to be disciples (students) and to learn the way Jesus taught his followers—around the dinner table!

In the Jewish scriptures, we read how God sealed the covenant with his People through a meal. The relationship of food and faith is brought to a whole new level when Jesus becomes our Bread and Wine, a sign of the Eternal Covenant with His family on earth! As a priest, you can imagine, I take my theology very seriously. Unfortunately, in today's fast-paced society, many of us have adopted a fast-food mentality. We have forgotten that food is supposed to do more than just fill our stomachs. So, as a priest who also loves food, I don't just want people to take theology more seriously, I want to encourage people to take the "theology of food" more seriously! And, thank God, people are listening.

Over the past year, I've had the opportunity to personally offer Grace Before Meals presentations to people around the world. No matter where I go, I see parents and children hungering for the same things: a deeper sense of what it means to be a family, a renewed sense of Faith, and more opportunities to celebrate love for one another.

I'm not saying Grace Before Meals is the answer to every hunger we have. But this movement, at the very least, asks the question: What are you hungering for?

The Grace Before Meals philosophy is making a difference in the lives of many families. And, trust me, I can't take credit for any of it. This movement is being supported completely by God. I like to think of myself as the young child in John's gospel who just happened to have some fish and a few loaves. As this story shows, if we place our small gifts and talents in Jesus' hands, he can make miracles! And Grace Before Meals has been somewhat miraculous for me and many others!

This movement encourages us all to consider what our gifts and talents are. Are we placing these gifts and talents in God's hands in order to feed the hungry in our world—beginning with those at our own dinner table?

Several students and family members joined me in the kitchen of Dr. Thomas H. Powell, president of Mount Saint Mary's University, for an evening of great food and conversation.

Remember, feeding each other is one of the greatest ways we can show love. Consider a romantic dinner where lovers feed each other; newlyweds stuffing wedding cake in each other's mouth; a mother breast-feeding her newborn; a father working long hours to earn bread for his family; and volunteers at the soup kitchen serving the homeless with a smile. All of these examples prove that *food is love*!

As you participate in *our* movement, I pray you see your family and relationships as gifts from God that nourish you in body, mind, and spirit. I also pray that *our* Grace Before Meals movement brings us to a deeper love for God as His Children who are fed from His table. Finally, I pray that as God's children, we will then be inspired to feed a world that is truly hungering for grace-filled meals until we reach that Heavenly banquet!

Fr. Leo Patalinghug

Celebrating Mother's Day with my sisters, Maria and Angelica, my father, Carlos, my mother, Fe, and brother, Carlos Jr.

*from my family
to yours...
Happy Feasting!*

INTRODUCTION

Grace Before Meals

RECIPES FOR FAMILY LIFE

So he commanded the skies above; the doors of heaven he opened.

God rained manna upon them for food; bread from heaven he gave them.

All ate a meal fit for heroes; food he sent in abundance.

PSALM 78:23–25

If food is one of God's bountiful blessings to His people, it only makes sense that the preparation of that food can also be a blessing, especially to our families. There are countless opportunities to teach and learn about God in every aspect of our relationship with food. From our earliest years, we can understand the miracle of growth as we sow seeds and watch them flourish under our watchful care, or prop a potato over a container of water and watch it sprout roots and leaves. As grandparents, we can pass on traditions flavored with secret recipes for the special cakes and pies that have been family favorites for longer than anyone remembers. Or perhaps we can tell the stories of times when God showed His goodness by providing "manna" for our family in times of trouble.

In between these two extremes of discovery and remembrance, the time spent in a kitchen preparing a meal as a family offers unmatchable opportunities to learn and talk about much more than measuring flour or chopping vegetables. Conversations come easily in a kitchen, and both parents and children often find it safer to have a heart-to-heart talk if they don't have to be eye-to-eye while they're doing it.

The inevitable shared successes and failures that come with the process of creating sauces and soufflés also serve a deeper purpose.

They shrink the gaps in relationships stretched by packed schedules.

This edition of *Grace Before Meals* was created especially for families. Without being "preachy" or boring, parents can use these themed meals—from the obvious, like Thanksgiving, to the less obvious, like World Day of the Sick—to provide food for the soul as well as the stomach. Along with short essays, scriptures, and menus, you'll find dozens of suggestions for transforming mealtime lessons into actions that respect children and teens, acknowledge their unique needs, and reinforce their connection to the family.

The best teachers, especially parents, never stop being students themselves. So it is our hope that you will be surprised by what you discover as you go through each chapter. Our prayer is that your own gifts and experience will be enriched as both you and your children learn how to prepare, serve, and enjoy meals that richly satisfy long after the meal is over and the kids have grown into adults.

Using This Book

Experiencing true grace before a meal is not limited to the prayer families say before they eat. It happens when you come together to cook, talk, and share blessings at your table! Here are a few hints to help make *Grace Before Meals: Recipes and Inspiration for Family Meals and Family Life* even more effective:

Satisfying Our Hungry Hearts

Each chapter begins with a brief passage from Sacred Scripture followed by a lesson or thought about the suggested event or holy day/holiday. From there, families have an opportunity to make the celebration happen by coming together to create not only a delicious meal, but great memories, too.

Let's Talk

This list of questions can help families start conversations about the things that matter most to them, namely, what each of you believes. Some feel that families should not talk about religion, sports, or politics at the dinner table. I wholeheartedly disagree! These proposed questions allow your family to talk without fear, but with love!

Let's Listen

God's Word is alive and enlivening! These Scripture references give families an extra opportunity to consider God's perspective on family life and holidays, or as some originally called them, "holy days." Some families may even want to begin their family meal with one of the suggested passages or use it as a meditation throughout the week. This section reminds us that God does speak to us in our hearts, so let's leave room for Him at our table.

Let's Cook

The proposed menus come from my experiences while traveling, dining with my family, friends, and parishioners, and experimenting to satisfy my own cravings. Don't feel obligated to use these exact menus in this exact order. Feel free to mix the recipes and ingredients based on your family's taste buds, cravings, and dietary restrictions. In fact, feel free to make a completely different meal for your family, but don't pass up the opportunity to share in the discussions. It is my hope that these recipes can inspire you to travel deeply in the journeys you all take in life and to experiment with your family's cravings as well.

Fun Facts

Fun facts make life fun! That's why we've highlighted some of our family-friendly ideas, cooking tips, and other fun facts. We hope you enjoy the colorful and easy-to-read format, because we want to help make your family experience fun, as a matter of fact!

Bon Appétit!

CHAPTER 1

The Most Uplifting Throwdown

ACCEPTING A CELEBRITY CHEF'S CHALLENGE

Brothers, I for my part do not consider myself to have taken possession. Just one thing: forgetting what lies behind but straining forward to what lies ahead, I continue my pursuit toward the goal, the prize of God's upward calling, in Christ Jesus.

PHILIPPIANS 3:13–14

Street talk gives the definition of a throwdown: It's a challenge, competition, and a chance to prove who is best. It's also the name of the hit Food Network show *Throwdown with Bobby Flay*. According to the show's opening credits, the world renowned chef sends a film crew to travel the country in search of cooks and chefs with notoriety for a particular dish or cooking style. The producer for this show lures the unsuspecting chef into filming what the person believes will be a segment of an episode on a future Food Network show. Little do they know they are being set up for a "throwdown" against one of the American "Iron Chefs." Bobby Flay, the star of the show, surprises the chef and challenges him to a cooking competition. The sparks fly with delicious foods, families, and fun!

I've watched this show for many seasons. I always felt terribly nervous for the unwitting opponents. I've cheered for those who won! I admired how the Food Network star humbly receives his losses. I am actually more impressed with how he humbly accepts his victories. Bobby Flay has always been a bit of an enigma to me. His Irish blood is uniquely infused with Southwest Tex-Mex spices! As a TV personality, he couples a strong and confident New Yorker with a gentlemanly quality, almost boyish at times. He's great on TV. He's the kind of man that everyone wants to meet. His cooking creations are exactly what everyone craves! You can see why this show is such a hit with food lovers and anyone who enjoys watching TV for good family fun competition.

The show is so engaging that I sometimes feel a part of it, to the point of envy for the chefs who had the incredible opportunity to meet a great chef and personality like Bobby Flay. Yes, I also get a little jealous of everyone who has the chance to taste the food! I've watched this show enough times that I've had my share of questions too: Are the contestants truly surprised? Are the judges really unaware of whose dish belonged to whom? What is it like for the people who actually get a chance to taste these cooking creations? How much filming is required for a weekly half-hour show? What does that food taste like? Little did I know that I would have the answer to all my questions!

On November 11, 2008, I received an e-mail from someone representing Food Network. I thought it was a joke. But a follow-up e-mail told me they were serious. It seems that someone at the network saw one of my cooking webshows and they were interested in exploring ways to film a segment about my cooking and my work with Grace Before Meals. They said they were developing an episode that features food topics presented on the Internet. As the host for the webshow, I felt comfortable, in fact excited, to share the mission of our movement with the Food Network. To prepare for this shoot, several conference calls with the producers had to be made. Everything had to be just right. Photos, e-mails, recipes, and more phone meetings. So much work goes into these shoots that I was feeling a bit overwhelmed, and even a bit discouraged. At one point I thought that this video shoot might not be God's plan for me, because we were having trouble finding time in our busy schedules. But the producers were encouraging, patient, and even a bit insistent that we somehow find time to film. They were genuinely excited, respectful of my work as a priest, and encouraging of the work of Grace Before Meals. They said that our Grace Before Meals message is an important one, and that it needs to be shared with a wider audience. This obviously motivated me to do what I could to help spread the message to help strengthen family relationships around the dinner table—just like Jesus did in the Last Supper and we do at every Mass. I felt a little bit like a missionary in a new field of evangelization. It was exciting, fun, and frightening at the same time.

The dish they wanted me to showcase was my "Fusion Fajitas"—a traditional South American dish that incorporates savory meats and grilled veggies, wrapped in either a corn or wheat tortilla. In order to make my fajita extra special, I created a marinade for the meat that celebrates the "International" aspect of my food and faith experiences, incorporating European ingredients with my Filipino background. The result was a "fusion" of flavors that still respected the traditional origins of this relatively simple dish. My hope was to hit the different taste buds of the palate. After a few attempts at creating the right blend of ingredients, I was very satisfied with the turnout, and so were the Mount St. Mary's seminarians who taste tested the final product. Truth be told, it was delicious! I was proud and excited to share this great family-friendly recipe with the Food Network. They liked it too!

After months of planning and waiting, the day for filming finally arrived. Day one of the shoot I was busy cooking and interviewing. Lighting had to be perfect, camera angles were taken into precise consideration, and enough bloopers on my part meant that we would have a few retakes. It was an amazing experience—one that left me excited and exhausted at the same time. But I needed to save my energy because day two of the shoot was only a few hours away, and I still had to cook enough of these fajitas for a large crowd that would gather to celebrate the Grace Before Meals message. I had already experienced traveling the country, spreading this message, and giving similar presentations to different church groups, agricultural departments, and family ministries, as well as on multiple news segments. Doing this presentation for the Food Network wasn't "difficult," but it would be a unique experience since I would be offering this message for a national audience. The pressure was on!

June 9, 2009, the second day of the filming, came quickly. It was a beautiful day, but the weather report threatened severe lightning and thunderstorms. Family and friends, however, stormed heaven with prayers. It couldn't rain because the filming was to take place in the outdoor backyard banquet tent of the Mount St. Mary's University president's home. He and his wife graciously offered the film crew their personal space and offered to host this "celebration" of faith, food, and family. The rain held. Prayer worked. God was on our side.

The day of filming was a bit like Thanksgiving. Family and friends came to celebrate! My good friend and cooking partner from my seminary days, Msgr. Christopher Nalty, traveled to Emmitsburg from the Archdiocese of New Orleans to offer me support. While he preferred to just sit back, watch, and support me in prayer, I put him to work by making him my grilling assistant. Tim Watkins, owner of Renegade, the production company that produces *Grace Before Meals*, brought several of his staff to make sure the filming went smoothly. His presence helped me to keep the movement's mission ever before me, especially since filming can make a guy very nervous. Family, friends, and Grace Before Meals supporters all came out, excited to be on TV and hungry to taste this special menu.

The day started off with a flurry of activity in setting up the tent for this celebration. My nieces and nephews were on hand to sing a few songs to get the crowd going. We all joined for a little prayer and then I was on. It was time to cook and

share the Grace Before Meals message with all of the invited guests—live and on TV.

All seemed to go as planned, until the producer pointed to me to look in the direction of what I thought was another camera. Instead, she was pointing for me to look in the direction of a very special guest who secretly and surprisingly broke through the crowd. I was staring at Bobby Flay— the star of his own show!

"Oh, Good Jesus!" Those were the words that came out of my mouth as I realized that Chef Bobby Flay was standing in front of the crowd, arms crossed, with a coy grin on his face. At that moment, I realized that the filming wasn't just about Grace Before Meals, my cooking, or my message. This chef superstar was there to issue me a "Steak Fajita Throwdown!"

"As God is my witness, I am not afraid. Bring it!" That was the best response I could muster. I was so nervous, I felt—for the first time—at a loss for words. My response was not measured or calculated. I had no time to prepare. I was truly surprised! I just had to act by faith, and not by "sight." Bobby Flay's presence truly blindsided

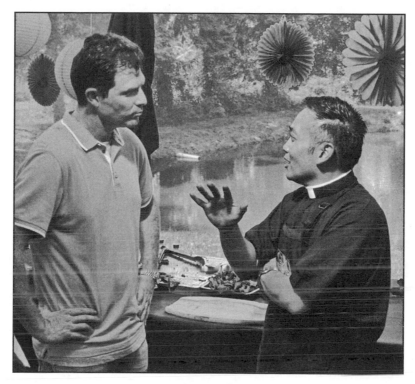

Bobby Flay and me

me. At the same time, he humbled me and honored me!

Without reducing faith to a cooking show, I must say this surprising moment in life required a response of faith. I was issued a challenge—a *big* challenge. Our faith, our lives, our families are constantly being issued *big* challenges. Are we ready for a throwdown? With God as our witness, we need not be afraid!

The responses we give to challenges in life are just as significant as the challenges themselves. I knew this throwdown would make me face my insecurities, thrill my sense of adventure, and humble my pride, because losing was a real possibility. And losing in front of millions of viewers can be very humbling. Such thoughts made my hands tremble! But I had no time to dwell on my fears. I had to do something important. I had to cut onions!

As "the show must go on," so must our lives, our families, and work—even in the midst of great challenges.

During the next few hours, it felt like my head was spinning. Extra cameras were brought in. New film crew with more lights and extended microphones popped out of nowhere. New people were brought in to help Bobby Flay, including his trusted assistants, Stephanie and Miriam, whom I had seen on TV and who were now in front of me cutting, mixing, and cooking. While I had to cut, prep, and cook more ingredients, the producers were interviewing me about how I felt. What was I thinking when I accepted a challenge from a culinary master? The most distracting part of all was the delicious aroma of Bobby Flay's food cooking on the grill!

Now I can say the experience left me in such awe that I had difficulty remembering all the delicious details. I remember how gracious Bobby Flay was to me, and all the guests at the event. I remember how tired I was after everything ended. I remember how the storm finally came, but at the right time, the moment the taping ended. I also remember who was declared the winner, but could not say anything until we would all watch it unfold on national TV.

On September 9, 2009, at 9:00 P.M. EST (that is, 9/9/09 at 9:00 P.M.), I watched the episode with my family, friends, and about three hundred guests who gathered in downtown Baltimore's famous Little Italy for an open-air block party and screening of the premiere. We laughed, we cried—well, at least my mother did—as we all proudly watched what many people posted on the blogs as, "the best *Throwdown* ever"! Of course, I cringed at hearing my own voice and watching my "silliness." But ultimately, I was filled with so much happiness and pride watching the seminarians serve the food and the happy faces of the families who came for the taping. I was reminded of Bobby Flay's winning personality, and was so grateful for his own humility to come to Emmitsburg, Maryland, and to bring national (and even international) attention to our grassroots movement.

But then came the moment of truth. The press, bloggers, and media, especially Catholic media, all wondered who had won. And, since I wasn't allowed to tell anyone, the tension was definitely in the air. We all roared with joy as I was declared the winner of the Steak Fajita Throwdown!

Shortly after the *Throwdown* episode, one of our Grace Before Meals staff checked the website statistics. In the month of September 2009, our website received over two million hits! It made me realize—our Grace Before Meals family is growing!

While we have been blessed with the national exposure by one of the great TV chef personalities out there, I realize that Grace Before Meals has a long way to go in meeting every family at an important place—their dinner table.

Challenges will be with us until the day we die. But in God's mind, each challenge is supposed to bring out the best in us. That's the message that I received from this incredible *Throwdown* experience. It's one that needs to be shared with every family, simply because sometimes the family struggles can unfortunately bring out the worst in us. The Grace Before Meals movement knows how difficult it can be, and that's why we're here to help. With God, even the most difficult throwdown can be an uplifting one. Every outcome of every challenge should reveal how God supplies the grace to make it through the seemingly impossible, including cutting onions when your hands are nervously shaking!

Let's Talk

Have you ever experienced anything so nerve-racking that it made you shake?
What was it and how did you survive it?

If you were given an opportunity to cook next to someone as talented as Bobby Flay, what would you cook and why?

Why is the media a necessary part of spreading a message of faith?
What do you think about religious people on "regular" channels doing something not so "churchy"?

If you had an opportunity to have your own show, what would you present, talk about, or show, and why?

Have you ever challenged someone in a competition? What was your intention in doing so?

What is the greatest challenge your family has ever faced? And how did you get through it?

How do you think God and prayers can help in competitions?

Let's Listen

John 14:1–4   Philippians 4:6   1 Peter 4:8–10

Let's Cook

Nearly every day, we all experience "throwdowns" to one degree or another. When preparing this meal, think about the throwdowns others face in life and how they compare to your own. Looking at your trials from a different perspective will help you savor both your meals and your blessings that much more.

Father Leo's Funky Fusion Fajitas

Serves: 4 to 6 | Prep Time: 2 to 4 hours (includes marinating) | Cooking Time: 25 minutes

1¼ pounds flank steak

MARINADE
2 garlic cloves, finely minced
¼ cup white wine
¼ cup soy sauce
2 tablespoons ketchup
1 teaspoon red pepper flakes
¼ cup red wine vinegar
¼ cup olive oil
1 cup dark brown sugar
2 teaspoons kosher salt
1 teaspoon cracked black pepper
1 teaspoon garlic powder
1 teaspoon ginger powder

HOLY GUACAMOLE
2 avocadoes, halved and pits removed
Juice from 1 lime
1 garlic clove, chopped
½ teaspoon salt
½ teaspoon black pepper
2 teaspoons minced parsley
2 teaspoons minced cilantro
4 teaspoons finely minced red onion
4 teaspoons olive oil

VEGETABLES
2 tablespoons olive oil
1 garlic clove, minced
½ red onion, sliced thinly
2 colored peppers, sliced into ¼-inch-thick pieces
4 scallions, chopped into ¼-inch pieces
2 to 4 tablespoons of the reserved marinade
Salt and pepper to taste

SCREAMIN' SOUR CREAM
½ cup sour cream
2 teaspoons hot sauce
½ teaspoon salt
¼ teaspoon freshly ground black pepper
1 teaspoon garlic powder

Tortillas

Use a fork and poke holes in the steak to tenderize. Place in a resealable plastic bag and set aside. In a bowl, combine all the marinade ingredients together and whisk until fully incorporated. Reserve ¼ cup of marinade. Pour the rest of the marinade in the bag with

[recipe continues on next page]

---

the flank steak and refrigerate for 2 to 4 hours.

To cook the steak, heat grill to high. Place steaks and turn down heat to medium. Cook for 7 minutes on each side and let rest for 7 minutes. When preparing to serve, cut thin strips against the grain of the meat.

To prepare the guacamole, remove the flesh from the avocadoes and immediately pour the lime juice on top to prevent the flesh from turning brown. Combine the rest of the guacamole ingredients and mash together with a fork. Set aside in the refrigerator.

To prepare the vegetables, heat olive oil and garlic in a pan over high heat. Add the vegetables and sauté for 2 to 3 minutes. Add the reserved ¼ cup marinade and cook for another minute. Season with salt and pepper. Take off heat and set aside.

To make the sour cream, mix together the sour cream, hot sauce, salt, pepper, and garlic powder and refrigerate until ready to use.

To assemble the fajitas: Spread 1 heaping tablespoon of guacamole over tortilla. Add 4 to 5 thin slices of meat. Add a few pieces of stir-fried vegetables. Top with sour cream. Pray and eat!

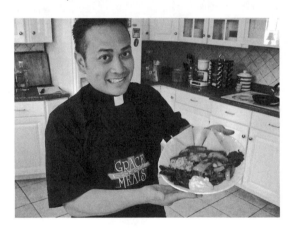

CHAPTER 2

Fresh Starts

So whoever is in Christ is a new creation: the old things have passed away;

behold, new things have come. And all this is from God, who has reconciled us

to himself through Christ and given us the ministry of reconciliation.

II CORINTHIANS 5:17–18

Happy New Year! Have you ever wondered why we make such a big deal out of New Year's Day? Even before there were marathon bowl games, Mummers parades, and downtown fireworks shimmering off skyscrapers, we welcomed in the new year with bells and toasts and a quick look back before we embraced the new year with all its possibilities.

Whether we realize it or not, our celebrations mark something far more important than a change in the calendar. They commemorate something that is unique to our faith and to American culture—the new day and the opportunity to live very differently than we have in the past.

The verse at the top of this page says a remarkable thing about God. When we tell Him the truth about ourselves, He reconciles us to Himself. He changes the course of our lives so that we are no longer turning away from Him but running toward Him. When we are adopted into His family, we're truly new creations. Think about it—when He looks at us after we have sought forgiveness, He sees us wearing Christ's robes, graced by His gift of salvation. Our old failures are forgiven. God gives us a fresh start. And as if that weren't enough, He promises us one fresh start after another, every time we ask, no matter how many times we ask. Beyond that, He asks us to become reconcilers ourselves.

He wants us to make that ministry our number one priority!

We demonstrate our understanding of God's reconciliation in our lives when we take a look at ourselves and decide there are some things we'd like to do differently. We might identify old habits we want to get rid of and new habits we want to develop. We might make a list of New Year's resolutions or a more comprehensive set of goals for ourselves and our families. We might decide to make changes in small steps, or we might be ready to turn a dream into a reality.

The wonderful thing is that we have the freedom to reinvent ourselves by truly becoming

> *The new year represents the opportunity to live very differently than we have in the past.*

ourselves. In our society, we applaud those who have overcome adversity of all kinds and worked to make their lives better. We do not believe in any kind of caste system. In fact, we are more likely to appreciate the "self-made" entrepreneur than someone who lives off wealth accumulated by an ancestor.

The same is true for growing up. In their tween and teen years, young people can be really hard on themselves. Sometimes they misread the learning process as an unchangeable assessment of their potential. The urging of parents, teachers, or coaches who see so much potential in their children can be heard as criticism. Teens may not yet grasp the greatness of God, His ability to take away every sin we bring to Him, and His power to keep us from those sins that seem to ensnare us. You can help your kids through this time by emphasizing the positives and the new opportunities they'll encounter in the years ahead. Everybody needs somebody to pay attention to their successes. Why not share your own resolutions for this year with your children? You can cheer each other on as you all work on becoming new people in the new year!

Let's Talk

If you were creating a reel of highlights from last year, what would be on it?

What experience was the most fun? What accomplishment made you the most proud?

If you could do one new thing this year, what would it be? What is standing between you and that goal?

How could you remove or move around those obstacles?

If you were writing goals or resolutions for your family, what would top the list?

What would be one step toward achieving it?

Do you know somebody whose life is very different now than it was five years ago?

How did that change come about?

If your parents decided to make big changes in their lives—like going back to school or moving to another part of the country—how would you respond? Why?

How do you think they might respond if you made a decision like that?

How would remembering God's policy to "forgive and forget" influence your response to somebody who let you down and then tried to make it right?

Let's Listen

Psalm 40   Jonah 3   Acts 9:1–31

Ephesians 4   1 John 2

Let's Cook

A menu for the new year should include some traditional favorites that reflect your region or your heritage. Add these familiar dishes to the new ideas here, and everybody is sure to remember the food and fun long after they've forgotten the scores of those "can't miss" games.

Slow-Roasted Champagne Pot Roast

Serves: 6 | Prep Time: 15 Minutes | Cooking Time: 60 Minutes

2 pounds roast or top sirloin
¼ teaspoon salt
1 teaspoon black pepper
4 tablespoons olive oil
3 garlic cloves, finely chopped
6 potatoes, peeled and cut into quarters
3 onions, chopped into quarters
6 carrots, chopped into 2-inch sections
2 cups leftover champagne (or substitute a
     white wine)
½ cup soy sauce
2 bay leaves
1½ tablespoons cornstarch
1 tablespoon warm water

Preheat oven to 375 degrees. Season roast with salt and pepper. Heat olive oil on high in large pan. Carefully place meat in pan and sear for 2 to 3 minutes on each side, creating a "grilled" look. Remove the roast and place in a deep baking dish.

In the same large pan, add the garlic, potatoes, onions, and carrots. Cook for 2 to 3 minutes, stirring the mixture every now and then. Add champagne, soy sauce, and bay leaves and cook for 1 to 2 minutes. Add salt and pepper to the liquid according to your taste.

Pour mixture over roast and cover dish with aluminum foil. Use a fork to poke a few small holes for steam to escape. Cook for 45 minutes to 1 hour, or until temperature of meat reaches 140 degrees.

After roast is cooked, let rest for 3 to 5 minutes before cutting. Place roast in center of large plate, placing the vegetables around it (removing the bay leaves).

To thicken the sauce for gravy, strain the liquid into a saucepan. In a separate bowl, mix the cornstarch with the water to create a thick, paste-like substance. Add to the sauce and stir attentively until thick.

Roasted Broccoli Spears

Serves: 6 | Prep Time: 10 Minutes | Cooking Time: 10 Minutes

4 cups water
2 cups broccoli florets cut into 3 or 4 equal
    pieces
3 tablespoons olive oil
2 garlic cloves, finely chopped
¼ teaspoon salt
¼ teaspoon pepper
¼ teaspoon red pepper flakes
1 cup seasoned bread crumbs

Preheat oven to 450 degrees. Fill pot or deep pan with water and bring to a boil. Add broccoli and cook until it turns bright green. Drain water and add olive oil, garlic, salt, pepper, and pepper flakes. Stir the broccoli so that all sides are coated with the olive oil. Remove from pot and place on a cookie sheet. Coat broccoli with bread crumbs.

Place baking sheet in oven (uncovered) for 7 to 10 minutes or until you see bread crumbs darken.

The celebration of the new year should start off with prayer. Putting our best foot forward requires first folding our hands in prayer!

CHAPTER 3

One More Gift

After their audience with [King Herod], [the Magi] set out. And behold, the star that they had seen at its rising preceded them, until it came and stopped over the place where the Child was. They were overjoyed at seeing the star, and on entering the house they saw the Child with Mary His mother. They prostrated themselves and did Him homage. Then they opened their treasures and offered Him gifts of gold, frankincense, and myrrh. And having been warned in a dream not to return to Herod, they departed for their country by another way.

MATTHEW 2:9–12

Does your family history have a story about a package that was received after the Christmas celebration was over? Maybe it was a box that got accidentally pushed under the sofa or the skirt of the tree. Maybe it was something that Mom saw during the year and put away but then forgot when the holidays finally arrived. Maybe it was a gift from someone far away that arrived long after it was supposed to because it got lost in the mail. Or maybe it was a gift nobody knew about that was discovered among a loved one's possessions after his or her passing. No matter what the reason, a late gift takes on special significance because it stands apart and represents the care the giver took in finding something they hoped would be just right.

That's especially true of the gifts the Magi brought to Jesus, even though they must have seemed very odd to the shepherds who had also made their way to that most holy of places, the manger where the infant Jesus lay. But Scripture tells us that no one rejected the gold, frankincense, and myrrh. Somehow, everyone gathered at the stable where Mary and Joseph had found shelter knew that this was no ordinary birth and no ordinary baby; those extraordinary gifts were, in fact, just right.

Each of those gift-givers experienced supernatural clarity. No wonder they all knelt down. They were in the presence of the King, and they knew it, for God had revealed what they surely would have missed. God had also guided their choice of gifts, just as surely as He had directed their search for Jesus and protected them by instructing them not to return to King Herod. The Magi's revelation of the Christ Child is called Epiphany. In our language, the word "epiphany" means a moment of sudden understanding or realization. Most moments of realization pale in comparison to the first Epiphany, but it helps to identify with the feeling that comes when we get past a single event and grasp the big picture.

Most of us will never experience a miraculous epiphany like the Magi had, but God has a gift like the one He gave them, prepared for each of His children. That gift is wisdom. The wisdom that God gives is so valuable that when God asked Solomon what he wanted more than anything, Solomon passed up riches and power and requested wisdom, so that he could be a good leader. God responded by giving Solomon great wisdom and the wealth he did not covet.

Wisdom is the very opposite of self-reliance. It comes when we acknowledge that, like the Magi, we need guidance. As parents, we must look

Wisdom comes when we acknowledge we need guidance.

29

ahead and anticipate God shaping our children and maturing them for His purposes. We need to look for the virtuous qualities they possess that can be encouraged and developed. Parents also need to remember that they weren't left out when the presents were distributed. God has the gift of wisdom for everyone who asks for it. He guarantees the fit because it's exactly what He picked out for each of us. Go ahead and unwrap it!

Jesus was given gold because He was a king, frankincense because He was a priest, and myrrh because He is the sacrificial Lamb of God who takes away sins.

Let's Talk

Did you ever receive a "late" gift? Why do you remember it?

Did you ever get a gift that you didn't think you'd like or use,
but it surprised you once you gave it a try? What was it?

Have you ever received something that seemed wonderful but turned out to be a big disappointment?
Why didn't it measure up?

If you could request any gift, no matter how big or expensive or
hard to obtain, what would you want? Why?

Do you think that people are only wise in their old age? Who is the wisest person you know?

What good would wisdom do you? When do you think it might be most useful?

If you could give each of your family members a special gift that would last them for a lifetime,
what would you choose? How do you think the recipients would respond?

Let's Listen

I Kings 3   Job 28   Proverbs 4

James 1:17   I Corinthians 1:4–9

Let's Cook

One way to include others in your kitchen conversation about God's storehouse of good things is to invite family and friends to your home and prepare a meal that's unexpectedly festive.

This sauce can be used on any seafood. Mix it with lump crabmeat for crab imperial—a Maryland favorite!

Imperial Salmon

Serves: 6 | Prep Time: 10 Minutes | Cooking Time: 15 Minutes

6 salmon fillets
½ teaspoon salt
½ teaspoon pepper
½ tablespoon olive oil
1 cup mayonnaise
¼ cup mustard
2 tablespoons soy sauce
1 teaspoon Old Bay Seasoning
    (or Chinese five-spice powder)
2 teaspoons fresh chopped dill (optional)

Preheat oven to 375 degrees. Season salmon with salt and pepper on fleshy side of the fillet. Heat olive oil in a nonstick pan. Place salmon in pan, skin side down, for 30 seconds to 1 minute. Flip it over and sear the other side for 2 to 3 minutes. (While searing the flesh side, you can easily scrape off the seared skin with flat tongs, a fork, or a butter knife.) Remove salmon and let rest on a baking sheet.

In a separate bowl, mix together mayonnaise, mustard, soy sauce, and Old Bay Seasoning or five-spice powder, creating a creamy sauce. Use a spatula or spoon to spread the sauce evenly, covering each of the salmon fillets. (Optional: Sprinkle fresh dill over the sauce.) Place the baking pan uncovered in oven for 10 to 15 minutes, or until the sauce turns a deep golden brown.

Cheesy Squash

Serves: 6 | Prep Time: 10 Minutes | Cooking Time: 15 Minutes

3 medium-sized yellow squash, cut into
¼-inch fillets
3 medium-sized zucchini, cut into ½-inch
fillets
4 tablespoons butter
½ cup olive oil
1 teaspoon dried oregano
½ teaspoon each salt and pepper
½ cup Parmesan cheese, freshly grated

Preheat oven to 400 degrees. Place veggie "fillets" on a baking sheet. Melt butter and heat with olive oil and oregano in a saucepan or in a microwave. Stir together and pour over the vegetables and mix all together so that each fillet is coated with the mix. Shake salt and pepper over all of the vegetables—both sides. Place in oven for 10 to 15 minutes.

After vegetables are cooked, remove from the oven and shake or shave fresh Parmesan cheese over them at the last minute. Serve this one hot!

*Celebrating
the Epiphany can
remind us that
Christmas doesn't last
one day, but every
time we celebrate
God's gifts to us!*

CHAPTER 4

Soups and Smiles

Then the righteous will answer him and say, "Lord, when did we see you hungry and feed you, or thirsty and give you drink? When did we see you a stranger and welcome you, or naked and clothe you? When did we see you ill or in prison, and visit you?" And the king will say to them in reply, "Amen, I say to you, whatever you did for one of these least brothers of mine, you did for me."

MATTHEW 25:37—40

Old-fashioned meatloaf. Homemade macaroni and cheese. Grandma's chocolate chip cookies. We have a name for dishes like these that remind us of our childhood or make us feel safe at home after a tough day out in the world. We call them comfort foods. It's a good term, but it's not quite so good a concept. The problem? It's all about us.

Comfort is not a do-it-yourself project. It's a do-for-others way of living that comes back to us in unexpected ways that feel better than pampering ourselves ever could. This idea runs counter to what we see in our magazines and hear on our televisions. It is not the message our sons and daughters are hearing. Taking care of others is such an alien concept in our self-centered world that it is crucial for us to show and tell our children the truth: "Looking out for number one" is not their responsibility—it's God's. God, in His perfect wisdom, gives us the responsibility to bring kindness to others.

Not everyone is called to a religous vocational ministry, but all of us, no matter our age or our circumstances, are called to pass on the love of Christ by caring for the people around us. Jesus could not have spoken more plainly on the subject. If we love Christ, we cannot ignore the suffering of those around us. Mother Teresa said that when she looked into the eyes of the suffering, she saw Jesus. Her example should inspire us to look beyond ourselves for the people God puts in our path.

If we love Christ, we cannot ignore the suffering of those around us.

You may be thinking to yourself that it was easy for Mother Teresa to find the needy in Calcutta, but where are the people your family can help? They might be as close as the elderly couple next door, the single mom you see in the after-school pick-up lane, or the family in your church with a child who has special needs. It could be a coworker who is recovering from an accident or the new family who just moved from across the country and doesn't have relatives nearby. It might be someone within your own family—a grandparent who puts up a self-sufficient front but has fewer friends and outside activities these days. There is someone. How do we know? God would not tell us to do something we cannot do. And what does it mean to show kindness? The answer to that question is laid out for us, too. We call it the Golden Rule. Kindness is giving others what we would want them to give us. And still better, to love as God loved us.

What would feel like kindness to you? The answers are endless. Look at the person you are about to serve; put yourself in his or her place. If you were new in town, wouldn't you welcome a basket with a homemade meal and a small gift, like a local coupon book or the names and numbers of the neighbors along with an invitation to an upcoming get-together? If you were responsible for a child who required round-the-clock care, wouldn't you welcome a gift of fresh-baked goods and the offer to run an errand or help out with home care so you could have a respite? If you were lonely, wouldn't you be pleased with unexpected visitors bearing the ingredients for an impromptu meal to share?

Your child may surprise you with his or her awareness of others' needs and willingness to care for them. Kids tend to speak candidly with friends and classmates and reveal situations that adults often struggle with alone. As you deliberately act out of kindness, remember that God is not only using you as His ambassador, He is using you to shape the character of your child and preparing both of you for future blessings. Trust His plan. Let Him take care of you and your family's needs while you make some hearty soup and deliver it with some crisp crackers and a big smile.

World Day of the Sick is generally on February 11, the feast of Our Lady of Lourdes, a shrine in France where countless miraculous healings have taken place.

Let's Talk

Think of the advertisements you've seen lately.

Which ones tell you that you deserve the product they're selling?

When you don't feel good, what makes you more comfortable?

When you visit someone in a hospital or nursing home, how do you feel?

What would make you feel more at ease?

If you faced a crisis, where would you look for help?

Why do you think some people don't pay attention when they see

a person who is obviously living on the streets?

How does it make you feel when you do something nice for someone who can't return the favor?

Let's Listen

II Kings 4   Psalm 69   Isaiah 58   Acts 20

Let's Cook

ARROZ CALDO
GRILLED CREAMY VEGETABLE SOUP
SIMPLE FRENCH ONION SOUP

These soup recipes provide you with a chance to help a friend in need. Your goal is to present them with healthful, tasty food in a way that demonstrates caring and thoughtfulness, not duty. When you deliver the meal, allow enough

> *To facilitate the cooking and reheating process, keep garnish (such as croutons, sour cream, chives, and cheese) in separate containers.*

time in your schedule so you can freshen the glass of water at the bedside or do some light cleaning before you go. Your small acts will mean more than you ever expected.

Arroz Caldo

HOT RICE, CHICKEN, AND GINGER SOUP

Serves: 4 | Prep Time: 10 Minutes | Cooking Time: 20 Minutes

2 chicken breasts, cut into ½-inch cubes
1 teaspoon salt, plus more to taste
1 teaspoon black pepper, plus more to taste
1 tablespoon vegetable oil
3 teaspoons fresh ginger, grated
2 garlic cloves, minced
1 medium onion, finely chopped
1 cup uncooked rice
7 to 10 cups boiling water (depending on how creamy you want your soup)
Tabasco sauce (optional)
2 scallions, minced

Season chicken cubes with salt and pepper. Heat oil in a large saucepan. Add ginger and garlic. Sauté. Immediately add chicken and brown on all sides. Add onion and continue to cook until onion becomes clear.

Add rice to the mixture and cook until rice becomes slightly colored. Add hot water one cup at a time so that the rice becomes creamy. This usually takes about 2 to 3 minutes. Continue to add water, and continue to stir. Salt and pepper to taste.

When rice is soft, the soup is cooked. The soup is generally served very thick, almost like porridge. To thin it out, just add a cup or two of hot water and be sure to season accordingly. Serve with a few splashes of Tabasco sauce and a sprinkle of scallions for garnish and extra flavoring.

Grilled Creamy Vegetable Soup

Serves: 4 | Prep Time: 15 Minutes | Cooking Time: 20 Minutes

1 cup carrots, chopped into ½-inch pieces
1 cup broccoli florets, chopped in half
1 cup zucchini, chopped into ¼-inch pieces
1 cup fresh tomatoes, chopped into ¼-inch pieces
1 medium white onion, minced
1 garlic clove, finely minced
3 tablespoons olive oil
½ teaspoon salt
¼ teaspoon pepper
1 teaspoon oregano
3 cups chicken or beef broth
2 tablespoons butter
1 tablespoon flour
1 cup whipping cream
4 teaspoons sour cream
2 cups croutons
1 tablespoon chives, chopped (for garnish)

Turn oven to broil. Place chopped and minced vegetables on a cookie sheet and season with olive oil, salt, pepper, and oregano. Place veggies on middle rack of broiler for approximately 10 minutes, or until caramelizing occurs. Remove and cook the other side of the veggies for 3 to 5 minutes.

Remove and place the vegetables and the natural juices in a food processor or blender. Use some of the broth to help the blending process. (If using a blender, you may be required to repeat this process a few times so as to not overload the blender.) In a pot over medium heat, melt butter and add flour, creating a roux. Add one cup of broth, stirring to thicken the roux and avoiding lumps. Add the pureed vegetables. Continue to add one cup of broth at a time, while mixing and tasting for consistency. Add whipping cream and continue to stir. Salt and pepper to taste. Drop heat to low, allowing flavors to simmer together for about 5 minutes.

Ladle into bowls and dollop with a teaspoon of sour cream in each bowl. Evenly distribute croutons around the sour cream and drop a pinch or two of the chopped chives for garnish.

Simple French Onion Soup

Serves: 4 | Prep Time: 10 Minutes | Cooking Time: 15 Minutes

2 tablespoons butter
3 medium-sized white onions, sliced in ¼-inch rings
1 quart beef or chicken broth
3 tablespoons sherry wine (optional)
1 teaspoon Worcestershire sauce
1 teaspoon salt
½ teaspoon pepper
2 cups croutons
4 slices provolone cheese

Preheat oven to 350 degrees. Melt butter in pot and add onions to sauté. Cook until limp. Add broth, sherry, and Worcestershire sauce. Bring to light boil. Add salt and pepper. Distribute broth and onions into four individual oven-safe bowls or four extra-large mugs. Fill each bowl ¾ full.

Top each bowl with ½ cup of croutons and place one slice of cheese over each bowl. Place bowls on top of a cookie sheet and put in oven for 7 to 10 minutes or until cheese begins to bubble or melt.

CHAPTER 5

Adjusting Focus

Filled with the Holy Spirit, Jesus returned from the Jordan and was led by the Spirit into the desert for forty days, to be tempted by the devil. He ate nothing during those days, and when they were over he was hungry. The devil said to him, "If you are the Son of God, command this stone to become bread." Jesus answered him, "It is written, 'One does not live by bread alone.'" Then he took him up and showed him all the kingdoms of the world in a single instant. The devil said to him, "I shall give to you all this power and their glory; for it has been handed over to me, and I may give it to whomever I wish. All this will be yours, if you worship me." Jesus said to him in reply, "It is written: 'You shall worship the Lord, your God, and him alone shall you serve.'"

LUKE 4:1–8

"It's a matter of perspective." How many times have you heard that when people are discussing a topic that's generating a range of opinions? The music of your youth was incessant noise to your parents. The out-of-style clothes you shoved to the back of your closet are the retro styles your teen prefers. The art you just don't get sets an auction record, leaving you to wonder if you can teach the dog to hold a paintbrush and create a similar "masterpiece."

Perspective has everything to do with how you and your family approach Ash Wednesday and the forty days of Lent. In some ways it seems like a long time between candy bars or T-bones or whatever it is you've decided to do without. That's the part that comedians play up when they joke about what people give up for Lent.

Lent certainly is a time to remember what Jesus went through during His forty days in the desert. He not only fasted, He also withstood Satan's challenges and taunting. We might be able to convince ourselves we're suffering when we observe Lent, but we know we will never come close to what Jesus endured.

So how can we make the most of Lent and use this time for the good of our family and our faith? If we shift perspectives, we might be surprised by what we can gain in just forty days. Surely we will be ready to celebrate the joy of Easter with new enthusiasm.

How can that be? Simplifying gives us time to pay attention to the essentials. Making a homemade soup instead of a roast allows us more time to share the day as we chop the celery or slice the potatoes that go into our family recipe. Spending less per serving with a meatless meal makes it easier to invite friends to stay for dinner. Shopping less saves time that can be used for conversations about whether your family might be happier if you had less, instead of putting all your energy into accumulating more.

Life is more than the accumulation of things. There is so much to gain when we opt for less.

These aren't questions with right or wrong answers, and it is likely that the conversations will go on for some time as you consider all that you have to be thankful for and how you might use your blessings for the good of others. Don't be afraid to raise these issues with your children. Even when they're pushing you for the latest sneakers and CDs, they know they live comfortable lives. Help them to understand that success in life is much more than the accumulation of things by showing them what they can gain when they opt for less.

A shift in perspective can help us make the most of the Lenten season.

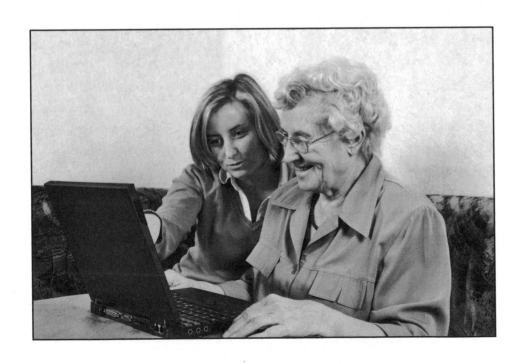

Let's Talk

Think about a time when you were really hungry. How did you feel?

Have you ever thought about what it would be like not to have food for weeks?

Sometimes people fast as part of a religious observance.

Why do you think they do that? What do they gain?

During his forty days in the desert, Jesus was tempted again and again, just like you.

How do you resist temptation?

If you and your family decided to change your lifestyle, what would you be willing to give up?

What would you definitely want to keep?

Have you ever done something nice for someone else and been surprised by

how good your kindness made you feel?

Lent lasts only forty days. What aspect of this observance

would you like to make a part of your whole year?

Let's Listen

Psalm 4   Jonah 2   Matthew 12   1 John 4

Let's Cook

The tradition of abstaining from meat products during Lent reminds us of the staple food in Jesus' time: fish. In fact, the Greek phrase "Jesus Christ, Son of God, Savior" creates the acronym "FISH" in that language. Eating fish is a reminder of Jesus!

> *Al dente is an Italian expression for how pasta is cooked. It means "to the tooth." The pasta should be taken off the stove while it is still slightly firm . . . Mushy pasta can be a "sin" in Italian cuisine!*

Meatless certainly doesn't have to mean tasteless. There are lots of vegetarian and meatless recipes your family will want all year round, but we think this menu will become a favorite.

Spaghetti Aglio e Olio
SPAGHETTI WITH GARLIC AND OLIVE OIL

Serves: 4 | Prep Time: 10 Minutes | Cooking Time: 15 Minutes

1-pound box thick spaghetti
4 tablespoons olive oil
1 anchovy fillet, mashed with a fork (optional)
2 garlic cloves, thinly sliced
2 pinches red pepper flakes
¾ teaspoon salt
¼ teaspoon black pepper
2 tablespoons parsley, freshly chopped (flat Italian parsley preferred)
½ cup fresh Parmesan cheese

Boil spaghetti until al dente (almost cooked but still a bit firm). Drain the pasta, but save about 2 to 3 tablespoons of the hot pasta water.

Heat oil in a pan, add the anchovy fillet and assist the breaking-up process with a wooden spoon or fork. Add the garlic and red pepper flakes to sauté (this process takes only 2 to 3 minutes maximum—you don't want to burn the garlic, so monitor the timing between the pasta and heating up the oil).

Carefully add the hot olive oil mixture to the pot and stir ingredients together. Add salt and pepper. Add the freshly chopped parsley and Parmesan cheese and mix together. Serve on individual plates, adding grated Parmesan cheese according to taste.

Lent is also a good time for Friday-night pizza with lots of fresh veggies, grilled portabella mushroom burgers, or corn chowder with a salad on the side.

Caprese Salad

Serves: 4 | Prep Time: 10 Minutes

2 large tomatoes
2 balls fresh water-packed
   mozzarella cheese
8 fresh basil leaves, minced
½ teaspoon salt
¼ teaspoon pepper
4 tablespoons extra-virgin olive oil
1 tablespoon balsamic vinegar

Cut each tomato and each piece of mozzarella into 4 equal rings. Place two rings of tomato on each plate, and then top each off with a slice of cheese. Sprinkle on some of the freshly minced basil (or 2 light dashes of dried basil). Add salt and pepper on each of the individual tomato and cheese rings. Mix the olive oil and vinegar together and spoon about 1 tablespoon of the mixture over each.

CHAPTER 6

Why Sacrifice?

SUGGESTED FOR THE FRIDAYS OF LENT

Rid yourselves of all malice and all deceit, insincerity, envy, and all slander; like newborn infants, long for pure spiritual milk so that through it you may grow into salvation, for you have tasted that the Lord is good. Come to him, a living stone, rejected by human beings but chosen and precious in the sight of God, and, like living stones, let yourselves be built into a spiritual house to be a holy priesthood to offer spiritual sacrifices acceptable to God through Jesus Christ.

I PETER 2:1—5

From the beginning of human history, God has instructed His people through the practice of sacrifice. It started when Cain and Abel, the sons of Adam, brought offerings to the Lord. Abel brought the best that he had, his first-born animals. Cain brought what was easy for him to part with from his garden. The Bible says God accepted Abel's gift but looked with disfavor on Cain's. Cain did not hide his anger, and God warned him not to let evil get the best of him. We know that Cain ignored that warning.

In contrast, Abraham trusted God even when he thought the sacrifice God required was his son, Isaac. When God saw Abraham's obedience, He blessed Abraham, first by sparing Isaac's life and providing a ram for the sacrifice, then by promising Abraham that his descendents would be a blessing to all the earth.

God does not ask us to sacrifice because He needs something from us. Instead, He wants us to understand the enormity of His love for us. Sacrifice is not about money. It is about everything. It is the willingness to give up your evening of relaxation to sit in a hospital waiting room with a neighbor whose husband has just had a heart attack. It is the decision to drive the old car for another year and put the extra money into a fund for your church's mission to orphans in Haiti. It is the willingness to visit your elderly aunt and assure her of your love even though she no longer remembers your name and may not remember your visit an hour after you've gone. Sacrifice is being alert to what God asks of you, and then doing it with confidence in His good plan.

Every Friday in Lent is a mini-commemoration of Good Friday. TGIF can have an entirely different meaning if we remember why Fridays are so important.

Your sons and daughters need help to understand the power and the price of sacrifice. They may resist the idea of doing without unless they see the purpose behind it. But when young people understand that willing sacrifices please God and bless others, they will be drawn into the circle of expectancy that faith creates as they watch their sacrifices be converted into someone else's smile.

During Lent, the practice of eating sacrificially on Fridays naturally encourages a family tradition of serving sacrificially on those days, too. Where could you give your time? Is there a project you could take on for an elderly neighbor or relative? Is there a family who would be encouraged by sharing your simple Friday meal? Do you have clothes you could share with a family whose children are outgrowing their budget? Can you give up tickets to that Friday game so a single mom can treat her kids to something she could not afford to give them herself?

Your sacrifices, big and small, during your observance of Lent will return to you and your family as new blessings when you consider the cost of Good Friday and the wonder of Easter.

Sacrifice is about more than money. It is about being alert to what God asks of you, and then doing it with confidence in His good plan.

Let's Talk

There's a famous Texas putdown: "All hat but no cattle."

How do you think that idea might apply to attitudes and acts of sacrifice?

What does it mean to live sacrificially?

Think about sacrifices that go beyond food and money.

Why do you think God is offended by some "sacrifices"?

What do you treasure? How could it be used sacrificially?

Have you ever considered the cost of God's sacrifice for you? Why did He do that?

How would you explain to a small child what it means to sacrifice?

Let's Listen

Genesis 22   1 Samuel 15:13–30   Mark 12:28–34   Romans 12

Let's Cook

Identifying with those in need can teach us a lot. In many parts of the world, as well as many homes in our country, foods we think of as staples are luxuries. As you take the time to put together a "frugal" meal, God will give you

Meals on Lenten Fridays should be more than cheese pizzas. They should be about creating flavors from simple ingredients.

creative ideas for making this sacrifice a truly special time of worship in word and deed.

Old Bay and Beer Shrimp with Herbal Crostini

Serves: 3 to 4 (appetizer) | Prep Time: 10 Minutes | Cooking Time: 15 Minutes for both recipes

SHRIMP
2 tablespoons butter
1 tablespoon olive oil
1 garlic clove, finely minced
2 tablespoons Old Bay Seasoning
1 tablespoon all-purpose flour
1 cup beer or ale
1 pound medium-sized shrimp, peeled and deveined
Juice of ½ lemon
1 teaspoon fresh parsley, minced

HERBAL CROSTINI
2 tablespoons mayonnaise
1 teaspoon garlic powder
1 teaspoon dried oregano
1 teaspoon dried parsley
1 teaspoon dried thyme
6 ½-inch slices of baguette

To make the shrimp, melt the butter and heat with the oil in a large sauté pan. Sauté the garlic. Whisk in Old Bay seasoning with flour and create a light roux. Add beer and bring to a light boil. Add shrimp and simmer until shrimp are pink. Add lemon juice and parsley. Mix together.

For the crostini, preheat oven to broil. Mix together mayonnaise, garlic powder, oregano, parsley, and thyme. Scoop ½ teaspoon of mayonnaise spread on each piece of bread. Place bread on a cookie sheet in the middle of the oven. Broil for 2 to 4 minutes, until the bread turns a light brown.

Serve the shrimp with the crostini.

Simple Festive Salad

Serves: 3 | Prep Time: 10 Minutes

1 bag prewashed mixed field greens
2 tomatoes, cut into wedges
Salt and pepper to taste
¼ cup extra-virgin olive oil
2 tablespoons lemon juice
¼ cup feta or blue cheese
¼ cup walnuts
½ cup dried cranberries

Lightly sprinkle mixed field greens and tomato wedges with salt and pepper. Whisk together the oil and lemon juice and add the blue cheese, walnuts, and cranberries. Mix together and pour over the salad. Toss the salad and add more salt and pepper to taste if necessary. Be sure to toss the salad again before serving, as the dressing ingredients tend to make their way to the bottom of the bowl.

This is a good time to remember that what matters most about our meals is not what's on our plates, but what's in our hearts as we cook and serve and share.

CHAPTER 7

Good Job!

RITES OF PASSAGE

His master said to him, "Well done, my good and faithful servant.

Since you were faithful in small matters, I will give you great responsibilities.

Come, share your master's joy."

MATTHEW 25:23

"You're my mother—you have to say that." Those all-too-familiar words are repeated every day by millions of kids who are worried about their looks, or their ability to play on the varsity team, or the likelihood that they'll have a date for the prom, or any of a hundred other challenges that make the middle school and high school years tough to navigate.

When their self-assessments are skewed toward "loser," young people don't quite know how to respond to a parental word of praise or encouragement that counters their critical evaluation. In their minds, anything positive has to be fiction. That's why a parent's attempt to help may be wrongly interpreted as pity or the expectation of failure.

There is, however, a way for parents to assure children of their confidence in them. The solution is so simple and obvious it is easy to overlook: Celebrate! Celebrate! Celebrate! Use every opportunity you can find to specifically tell your teen what is going right. This might take some getting used to because parents are more habituated to spotting the undone than the done, but the effort will pay off.

Find something to praise every day and point it out. Start the day with a casual remark like, "I think that shirt looks good on you," or "I'm looking forward to going to your game this afternoon." Individually, these remarks don't carry much weight, but cumulatively they convey that you are paying attention to your teen, and you like what you see. Bit by bit, these positive messages wear away negative self-perception and build a sense of worth.

Use the student council campaign, the learner's permit, the appreciative thanks from the

> *Both milestones and everyday events can be cause for a little celebration and a lot of affirmation.*

neighbor whose lawn got mowed, the first driver's license, the completed term paper, the science fair project that made it to school in one piece, or success in a game or on the stage as a reason to add a dessert to dinner or make a favorite meal. Every time you take note of a life mile-marker or a sign of progress and maturity, you are inoculating your son or daughter against the moments of despair that often make him or her deaf to the very same message. Accenting the positive at a moment when there is tangible proof of accomplishment provides an argument-free situation in which parents and other family members can express their pride, first in the child and then in the accomplishment.

You're not independently saying you think your daughter will make a good driver, you're repeating the opinion of the examiner who handed out the passing test grade. You're not exaggerating your son's intelligence, you're happily noting where he landed in the national percentile for students who also took that achievement test. You're not insisting that you gave birth to a future

Let your kids
know you're willing
to settle for less
drama in exchange
for a sincere hug.

Academy Award winner, you're saying that you will be an enthusiastic part of the audience on opening night at the school play.

As you work together to make a special just-for-us family meal, consider the possibility that you are creating a tradition that your children and their future spouses will use to mark their children's successes. Your grandchildren will always know what you are telling your children now: Their very existence, not their accomplishments, is a reason to have a party every day.

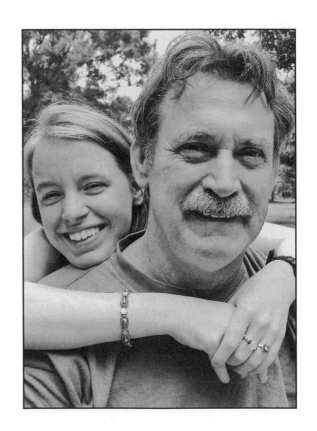

Let's Talk

Did your grade school teacher use gold stars? How did it feel to get one?

How did it feel when you didn't get one?

How did you form your opinion of yourself as an athlete?

What could change that opinion?

Some youth sports leagues give trophies to everybody on every team, while others limit awards to their champions and stars. Which approach do you think is most helpful to players? Why?

Look at your friends' families.

Do you see contrasting ways of handling accomplishments and challenges?

Have you ever helped a small child perfect a skill like walking or learning the alphabet?

How did you encourage him or her to keep trying when the going got tough?

If celebration suppers become regular events at your house,

what do you want to celebrate next?

Let's Listen

Zephaniah 3:14 20   Matthew 25.14–30   Luke 15:11–32   II Corinthians 8

Let's Cook

POACHED SALMON
WITH CREAMED ASPARAGUS DRESSING

"This calls for a celebration" can become one of your family's favorite expressions when you decide together that you aren't going to let each other's accomplishments, both tiny and terrific, slip by unnoticed. This menu expresses your willingness to do something extra on those special occasions.

Poached Salmon with Creamed Asparagus Dressing
Serves: 6 | Prep Time: 15 Minutes | Cooking Time: 20 Minutes

POACHED SALMON
1 teaspoon salt
½ teaspoon black pepper
6 individual-portion salmon fillets
3 tablespoons olive oil
2 cups orange juice
1 cup white wine
3 tablespoons honey or syrup
2 bay leaves
2 garlic cloves, thinly sliced

DRESSING
10 to 15 fresh asparagus stalks
1½ to 2 cups sour cream
Approximately ½ teaspoon salt
Approximately ¼ teaspoon black pepper
1 to 2 teaspoons fresh dill, minced

Salt and pepper salmon on both sides. To a deep pan, add olive oil, orange juice, wine, honey or syrup, bay leaves, and garlic slices. Cook over medium heat until liquids begin to simmer. Add salmon and poach for 5 to 7 minutes on each side uncovered.

Remove salmon and let rest away from the liquids. Continue to cook liquids until reduced by half. The thick liquid, after straining, serves as a nice sauce on which to place the salmon.

To prepare the dressing, cut or break off the woody part of the asparagus stems. In a deep pan, add hot water and let it come to a boil. Add asparagus and cook until it turns bright green and tender (not too soft). Remove asparagus immediately and place in a food processor with the sour cream. Add salt and pepper to taste and blend to a creamy light green consistency.

Use a serving spoon to top off the poached salmon with dressing. Sprinkle fresh dill on top for garnish and extra flavor.

CHAPTER 8

Heat and Light

When the time for Pentecost was fulfilled, they were all in one place together....

And they were all filled with the Holy Spirit and began to speak in different tongues,

as the Spirit enabled them to proclaim.

ACTS 2:1—4

What kind of power could change a small group of frightened and confused men and women into fearless witnesses for their faith? The same kind that is available to you and every believer today. Christ Himself promised that power when He commissioned the seventy-two who went before Him to proclaim the Good News of salvation. He promised that power again after the resurrection when He told His disciples to stay in the city until He sent what the Father had promised so that they would be "clothed with power from on high."

That power arrived on Pentecost, and ever since that day the presence or indwelling of God Himself in the person of the Holy Spirit comes to everyone who becomes a new creature in Christ. The Apostle Paul tells us in his letter to Rome that apart from Christ, we are dead in our sin. But God regenerates us and gives us a new heart when He draws us to Christ. Paul calls this the "free gift of God." Regeneration is the work of the Holy Spirit who takes up residence in that new heart, making a new life possible. Every believer has been touched by the Holy Spirit.

Every believer depends on the Holy Spirit for the power to live a life that reflects Christ and rejects evil.

In their new lives, the disciples were radically changed. They were empowered by the Holy Spirit to follow Christ's commission to go out into the world and proclaim God's truth. They were able to speak in languages they had never learned and be easily understood by the people around them. They were able to preach boldly, even when threatened with death, and they were able to live in a way that amazed people and made them want that same power.

The cynics of the day accused the disciples of drunkenness, but the Apostle Peter boldly corrected them. Because of the power of the

> *Every believer depends on the Holy Spirit for the power to live a life that reflects Christ and rejects evil.*

Holy Spirit, Peter was a changed man, no longer afraid to be publicly identified as a follower of Christ. He now welcomed the opportunity to address the thousands who gathered. Peter reminded the doubters in the crowd that it was morning; no one had been drinking. What they were witnessing was the fulfillment of Joel's prophesy that "God would pour out His Spirit on His people; He would fill them with His presence." Peter told the crowd that Jesus Christ was alive and that He was both Lord and Christ. His audience listened, wanting to know what they should do. Without hesitation, Peter told them to repent and be baptized so they, too, could receive new life and the presence of the Holy Spirit. Peter said that God's promises were for all those He called to Himself. Peter's message got through. That day, three thousand people were moved from spiritual death to life. As the disciples and the growing band of new believers continued to share their faith, their numbers increased daily.

Now we are a part of that band of believers. We are in that line that stretches from the first Pentecost to today. On this very day, new believers will be called to Christ by the power of the Holy Spirit. It is the Spirit who empowers us, all of us, to share our faith. The Holy Spirit provides security at moments when we would otherwise be afraid. He gives peace when our human impulse is to panic. He provides boldness when we would be timid. The Holy Spirit is the fire that melts our icy hearts. He is the light that finds us and leads us when we cannot see. He is our perfect comfort when we ache. The Holy Spirit is the embodiment of Christ's promise that He would never leave or forsake those He redeemed.

Has your faith been a little flat? Ask the Holy Spirit to fill you with His presence. Do you worry about the challenges of life, especially the surprises of parenting? Ask the Holy Spirit for confidence. Are there people you love who are cold toward faith? Ask the Holy Spirit to give you the boldness the disciples had on Pentecost. Go ahead and ask. The presence of the Holy Spirit is not restricted to others. It is your birthright as a believer and your gift from on high.

> *Do you worry about the challenges of life, especially the surprises of parenting? Ask the Holy Spirit for confidence.*

Seminary class picture with the late Pope John Paul II, including former rector Archbishop Timothy Dolan (far left) and me to the Pope's left.

Let's Talk

Why do you think Jesus promised the Holy Spirit to believers?

Do you feel believers in the twenty-first century can understand what Pentecost was like?
Why or why not?

Some people use the term "Holy Ghost" when referring to the Holy Spirit.
How would you help a child understand this term?

Does your family history include someone like the Apostle Peter or the Apostle Paul
whose life was turned around by faith and the power of the Holy Spirit?

If you were to ask the Holy Spirit for one thing today, what would it be?

When you think about having conversations with unbelievers, does the Holy Spirit's
promise to supply the words you need make you more comfortable?

Let's Listen

Joel 3   Mark 16   Acts 2

1 Corinthians 14   Hebrews 2

Let's Cook

Pentecost marks the point when the Gospel began spreading to all nations. It's all about energy and enthusiasm and power. A menu to celebrate the arrival of the Holy Spirit should be rich in flavors, even unfamiliar ones. If you have invited guests to

Try something new! Fusion foods combine various ethnic styles to create surprising and bold flavors.

share your meal, ask the Holy Spirit to use the time together as an opportunity for you to talk about your faith and how your life is different because the Holy Spirit is at work in you.

Cola Pork Skewers

Serves: 6 | Prep Time: 3 Hours (including marinade) | Cooking Time: 20 Minutes

3 to 4 pounds pork butt, cut into 1-inch cubes (aim to have 6 to 7 cubes per skewer)
1 tablespoon salt
½ tablespoon pepper
1 can dark cola drink, flat
½ cup soy sauce
6 tablespoons ketchup
3 bay leaves
5 garlic cloves, chopped
6 tablespoons olive oil
12 to 14 skewers (wooden or metal)

Season pork with salt and pepper. In a glass or nonreactive bowl, prepare a marinade by mixing together the flat cola, soy sauce, ketchup, bay leaves, and garlic. Add the pork to the marinade, cover, and let sit for at least 3 hours in the refrigerator.

When ready to cook, soak wooden skewers in water so they don't burn. Preheat grill. Skewer the meats, adding 6 or 7 cubes to each skewer. After all the skewers are in place, drizzle a little olive oil over them. When grill is ready, place skewers directly over medium heat, turning every 3 to 5 minutes on each side. This dish tastes great with sticky white rice.

Sweet Asian Slaw

Serves: 6 | Prep Time: 35 Minutes

6 tablespoons soy sauce
2 tablespoons rice wine vinegar (or plain
    distilled white vinegar)
1 cup mayonnaise
¼ teaspoon hot chili powder
4 tablespoons fresh cilantro, chopped
4 tablespoons fresh flat-leaf parsley, chopped
½ teaspoon pepper
½ head cabbage, finely shredded
    (approximately 6 to 8 cups)
3 carrots, shredded
2 oranges, peeled and sliced (or 2 small cans
    of mandarin oranges, drained)
½ cup cashews

In a large bowl add soy sauce, vinegar, mayonnaise, chili powder, cilantro, parsley, and pepper. Whisk together. Toss the cabbage and carrots into the sauce. Cover bowl with plastic wrap and let sit in refrigerator for about 20 to 30 minutes. Immediately prior to serving, mix in the oranges and cashews to add another level of flavor.

Alternate meal idea: Celebrate by preparing fondue or a flaming dessert to symbolize the fire the Holy Spirit ignites in our lives.

CHAPTER 9

Turning the Table

SUGGESTED FOR MOTHER'S DAY

Her children rise up and praise her; her husband, too, extols her: "Many are the

women of proven worth, but you have excelled them all." Charm is deceptive

and beauty fleeting; the woman who fears the LORD is to be praised.

PROVERBS 31:28–30

It's hard to imagine now, but it took an act of Congress in 1914 to make Mother's Day a national celebration. Thanks to all the gentle reminders, flower sales on Mother's Day are double what they are on Valentine's Day. The day is a record-setter for long-distance phone carriers, and it generates the sale of 155 million individual greeting cards, a number that doesn't even include those one-of-a-kind construction paper originals. No one keeps statistics on how many Mother's Day cards are tucked away in drawers and scrapbooks, but it would be safe to assume that number is in the billions.

A mother does not expect a lot of attention for her work. She knows it's a round-the-clock

If Jesus celebrated Mother's Day, what would He do special on this day?

assignment that will continue in some form until the day she dies. And if her own mother is no longer living, a mother knows her influence will last beyond her lifetime, just as her own mother's has for her.

A mother's job description often seems to focus on tasks like diaper changing, laundering, chaperoning, providing medical care, monitoring homework, supervising chores, cleaning, shopping, scheduling, waitressing, gift wrapping, caring for pets, and so on and so on.

That's all true, but the real role of a mother is not about tasks. It is about the intangibles of caring in a way that is truly unique. Mothers start loving their children long before they ever see them. They love the very idea of being a mother, and long to hold their child from the moment they know he or she is on the way. This is not simply biology; it is as true of adoptive mothers as it is of mothers who give birth. Children do not grow under their mothers' hearts. They grow in them.

Love is expressed in as many different ways as there are mothers and children. You see it on refrigerator doors where artwork and grade reports are posted for everybody to see. You hear it at soccer games and school concerts, where it is easy to determine which fan belongs to which "star." You feel it when you catch the look of a mother as she watches her child during those milestone moments that she helped make possible.

Because a mother's priority is others, she will protest that no one "should make a fuss" for Mother's Day. She will excuse her husband's failure to acknowledge the day by saying she's not his mother, though she will probably purchase a card for him to send his mother. She will understand any reason a child offers for not having time to send a card or make a call. After all, she's Mom, and she always looks for the best in her children, even when no one else can see it.

When we think about how much our mothers love us, one day to celebrate them hardly seems like enough. So even though they will tell you not

> *The real role of a mother is about the intangibles of caring in a way that is truly unique.*

64

to, make this day as special as you can. Don't worry about spending money. The gifts that mean the most to a mother don't cost a penny. Find a sheet of paper and write a thank-you note. Look around the house and find a project like cleaning out the hall closet or straightening up the family room that you can do without being asked. Offer to take a walk with your mother so you can catch up with each other. Ban her from the kitchen and the laundry room for an entire day, and hand her a book you've checked out of the library for her to enjoy. Think of something she does out of love for you, and do it for her. Don't be surprised if she cries a little. Moms are like that.

Set the tone with a surprise breakfast. Place a note or a prayer card on the tray or by Mom's place at the table.

Let's Talk

What is your favorite thing about your mother?
Does she know that?

What does she do that drives you crazy? Why does it drive you crazy?

Compared to other mothers you know, is your mom more or less strict? Is that a good or bad thing?

What makes your mother laugh?

Do you know what your grandmother was like as a parent?
How do you think she influences your mother?

Solomon demonstrated his wisdom when he settled a dispute between two women who both claimed to be the mother of a baby. He recommended that the child be divided in half. Why?

Which of your mother's traits do you hope to bring to your own parenting?

Let's Listen

Exodus 20:12   Proverbs 31:10–31   Isaiah 66:13

John 19:25–27   II Timothy 2:1–5

Let's Cook

It wouldn't matter if the toast were burnt and the coffee spilled a little, any meal for Mom will be welcomed with a smile. This menu is not overly complicated, so everybody in the family (except Mom!) can help in its preparation and be in on the surprise when it's served. Go ahead and use the good china!

This fancy breakfast sandwich is simple to make, but the result is a one-plate meal that includes all the favorite breakfast flavors!

Simple Monte Cristo

Serves: 1 | Prep Time: 10 Minutes | Cooking Time: 15 Minutes

2 eggs, beaten with 2 teaspoons water
1 teaspoon vanilla extract
3 pieces white bread, crust removed
4 slices cooked ham
2 thin slices Brie cheese, casing removed
    (or sharp provolone cheese slice)
1 cup bread crumbs
2 tablespoons butter
Maple syrup, slightly warmed

Beat together eggs with water and vanilla extract. Lightly coat both sides of each piece of bread in the egg mixture.

Assemble a simple triple-decker sandwich by placing 2 slices of ham and a thin layer of cheese between each piece of bread. Put sandwich together and cut diagonally to make 2 small triangles.

Dip each triangle of the sandwich on all sides into the batter once again, and coat all sides of sandwich in bread crumbs. In a nonstick frying pan, melt butter over medium heat and place the sandwich flat in the pan for approximately 1 to 2 minutes. Do this on each side. The egg batter around the sandwich edges should also be cooked; use tongs to hold the sandwich together while allowing the edges to cook for about 30 seconds on each exposed side. Drizzle the sandwich with warm maple syrup.

Mother's Day is not a religious celebration, unless you see your mother as a gift from God!

With my mother, Fe,
at my college graduation.

Breakfast Berries

Serves: 1 | Prep Time: 5 Minutes

½ cup sweetened condensed milk
½ cup evaporated milk
¼ teaspoon fresh mint leaves, finely minced
½ teaspoon fresh lemon zest
¼ cup fresh strawberries
¼ cup fresh blueberries (or any other fresh berries)
A few sprigs of mint (for garnish)

Combine condensed milk, evaporated milk, minced mint leaves, and lemon zest, and stir. Combine berries and milk mixture together. Serve with a sprig of mint for garnish.

CHAPTER 10

Burgers and Blessings

This is my commandment: Love one another as I love you. No one has greater

love than this, to lay down one's life for one's friends.

JOHN 15:12—13

There was a time in the not-too-distant past when families would take a picnic to the cemetery once or twice a year and spend the day caring for the family plot and reminiscing about relatives. In those cemeteries, many graves had a special tribute: a small United States flag signifying military service. Memorial Day has its roots in the custom of honoring the fallen with those flags on Decoration Day.

Flags are still put out each May in our national military cemeteries like Arlington, where there is a wreath-laying ceremony at the Tomb of the Unknowns. Flags are also displayed in communities where there are active veterans' groups. But increasingly, Memorial Day is associated with a three-day weekend and the start of the summer vacation season. Families can make sure the meaning of the day is not lost to them or their neighbors by teaching the significance of Memorial Day as part of their celebration.

Taking the time to consider the cost of freedom and the bravery of those who are called to military service is not a political statement. In fact, the freedom to have opposing views and express them without fear is one of the values our military defends. Our military history is marked by battles fought to liberate people and protect them from tyranny, not to gain territory or impose our authority. Memorial Day honors those who were willing to leave behind their comforts so that others might be helped. Their goal was peace, not punishment. They were not anxious to die, but they acknowledged that risk when they took on the responsibility. Our heroes are born not of conquest but of compassion.

Because of the terrible things they witnessed, many of our living military heroes have been reluctant to talk about their war experiences. It has taken the work of interviewers like Tom Brokaw to give us a true picture of those who served in World War II. Journalists have extensively covered more recent wars, and the bravery of those who have risked or even sacrificed their lives to protect others is now widely documented. The more we know, the more we understand why it is right to preserve the true purpose of Memorial Day and make sure our children understand the human cost of the freedoms they know.

Memorial Day honors those who were willing to leave behind their comforts so that others might be helped.

Your observance need not feel like a funeral— far from it. This is a time to savor what has been secured for you, including the fun of filling the backyard with family and friends to enjoy the first barbecue of the season. But start the day with a prayer and by hanging your United States flag from your porch or flagpole and placing smaller flags on your table. Do a little research on local Medal of Honor winners or military heroes. Find out about military veterans in your own family.

You may be surprised to discover that the reason an elderly aunt never married was not because she was never asked, but because her fiancé was a casualty in the Normandy invasion or was aboard a ship that was hit by enemy fire. Your own family history may provide reasons to make Memorial Day a more personal holiday celebrated not just with burgers but also with a prayer.

Your own family history may provide reasons to make Memorial Day a more personal day.

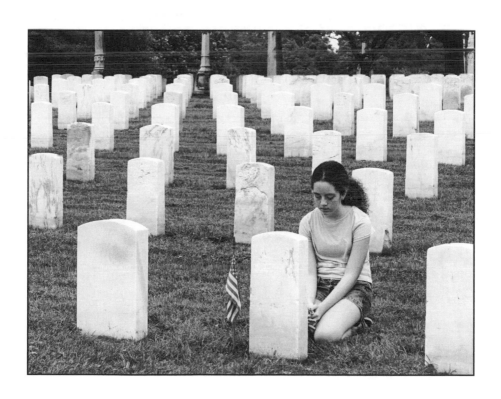

Let's Talk

Which freedoms do you most appreciate?

What do you consider worth defending, even worth dying for?

Do you have family or friends in the military right now?
Would you consider military service as an option for yourself?

We currently have an all-volunteer military.
What are the pros and cons of that policy?

In some parts of the world, teens are willing to become suicide bombers, and their parents take pride in that.
How would you attempt to change the mind of someone who had decided to become a suicide bomber?

The members of some religious groups are pacifists; Quakers and Mennonites are two examples.
How did the members of those groups fulfill their military obligation when they were drafted?
Was that appropriate or a violation of their convictions?

Let's Listen

Numbers 10:9   I Chronicles 12   Psalm 106:3   II Timothy 2

Let's Cook

This menu transforms the humble hamburger into a gourmet dish and your backyard into the neighborhood's favorite bistro. But before you sit down to eat, take a few moments to express your gratitude for those who have served our country and to pray for the protection of all those who serve today.

Make the chef's work as easy as possible by preparing ingredients in advance and using baskets or trays to get everything out to the grill area in as few trips as possible.

Burgers with Four Separate Toppings

Serves: 4 | Prep Time: 15 Minutes | Cooking Time: 10 Minutes

BASIC HAMBURGER MEAT (PREPARATION)

1 pound ground beef
1 teaspoon salt and pepper
1 packet onion soup mix (or 1 medium onion, finely chopped with 1 teaspoon garlic powder)

Combine all of the ingredients, using your hands to incorporate all of the flavors. Divide the ground beef into four burger patties and follow the instructions for each burger!

BURGER #1: BLUE CHEESE AND BARBECUE SAUCE BURGER

2 tablespoons barbecue sauce
2 tablespoons blue cheese (or Monterey Jack), crumbled

Combine the barbecue sauce with the crumbled blue cheese in a bowl. Use ½ of this combination and mix with one of the hamburger patties. Reshape the meat into a hamburger patty and cook on a grill for about 4 to 5 minutes on each side. When burger is cooked, top with the remaining mixture for a messy but tasty treat!

[recipe continues on next page]

BURGER #2: SWEET GINGER SOY BURGER

2 teaspoons brown sugar
2 tablespoons soy sauce
1 teaspoon fresh lemon juice
¼ teaspoon ground ginger powder

Combine all the ingredients and heat in a pan over medium heat until flavors are fully incorporated. Use ½ of this combination and mix with one of the hamburger patties. Reshape the meat into a hamburger patty and cook on a grill for about 4 to 5 minutes on each side. When burger is cooked, top with the remaining mixture, or brush onto the bun for extra flavor!

BURGER #3: PIZZA BURGER

2 tablespoons butter
½ onion, chopped
¼ teaspoon garlic powder
4 tablespoons tomato sauce
¼ teaspoon salt
3 pinches black pepper
2 to 4 pepperoni slices, finely chopped
2 tablespoons mozzarella cheese, grated

Melt butter in a saucepan and sauté onion and garlic powder together. Add tomato sauce and cook for about 3 to 4 minutes. Season with salt and pepper, stir, and set aside. Use ½ of this combination and the pepperoni slices and mix with one of the hamburger patties. Reshape the meat into a hamburger patty and cook on a grill for about 4 to 5 minutes on each side. Pour the rest of the sauce over the hamburger and top with cheese. Let this cook until cheese is melted.

BURGER #4: CALIFORNIA AVOCADO BURGER

1 avocado
Juice of ½ lime
¼ teaspoon salt
2 pinches black pepper
1 pinch garlic powder
1 teaspoon fresh cilantro, chopped
3 tablespoons sour cream

Cut avocado in half and spoon out the flesh into a bowl. Add lime juice, salt, pepper, garlic powder, cilantro, and sour cream. Using a fork, mash all of the ingredients together until you have a guacamole-style mix. Cook a burger patty and top with 1 ½ teaspoons of the mixture. Use the rest as a dip for potato or tortilla chips!

CHAPTER 11

Just Like Dad

Fathers, do not provoke your children to anger,

but bring them up with the training and instruction of the Lord.

EPHESIANS 6:4

Could there be a more important assignment than that of father? It is the relationship intended to give even the youngest child his or her first glimpse of what God Himself is like. The qualities of a loving father reflect those of our Heavenly Father. Human fathers guide and shape their children In ways that will assure them the spiritual quality of life God intends

Regardless of their personal gifts, fathers are expected to be able to do an amazing array of tasks. They need to assemble everything from swing sets and bunk beds, to half-pipes and doll houses. They have to fix anything they're presented with and, if possible, make it look easy so their child has bragging rights when the playground conversation turns to who has the best dad. They should be able to look at math homework and explain how to do it better than the teacher did. And they should have a schedule that allows them plenty of time to coach Little League or be a Scout leader.

Dads also have the tough job of setting limits. This is so difficult to do well that the Apostle Paul reminds fathers not to be harsh as they make and enforce the rules. They are to look to the Father and place their emphasis on training and instruction that brings their children close to God. Even the most outwardly compliant child will be angered by a human father whose manner of discipline is alien to the ways of the Heavenly Father, and that anger may lead to great pain for the entire family.

A father who commits to modeling God before his family will want to know God well. He will be a man of prayer, seeking the wisdom, patience, and love that God exhibits toward His children. He will not let his children give in to fear. Instead, he will be right there with them as they face down fears and conquer them. He will not indulge their selfish interest in their own comfort. He will teach them to see and care for the needy around them so that they might better appreciate all they receive from him. He will prepare his children for their own marriages by following the biblical instruction to love their mother like Christ loved the Church. He will give them a clear understanding of what really matters by arranging his schedule to show that faith and family are higher priorities than wealth and pleasure. In turn, his children will bless him for teaching them what God is like.

It is a sad reality that in our society many children are growing up in homes without a human father. But it is wrong to call them fatherless. God has given a special promise to these children and their mothers. He says that *He* will be their Father, and *He* will sustain them. They are not alone, and they are not unloved. One of the ways God fulfills His promise is by bringing godly men into their lives,

> *The qualities of a loving father reflect those of our Heavenly Father.*

men who are equipped to mentor, counsel, and encourage. These role models may be in a child's life for many years, or God may send them for a special task. No matter what their specific role, they bring with them blessings and tangible proof that God is true to His word. Father's Day is the perfect occasion to acknowledge fathers and fatherly figures and let them know how important their influence has been.

Even though Father's Day is not a religious holiday, you can show your father how much you consider him a gift to your family by giving him a special gift. As much as dads appreciate ties and shirts, what they really enjoy is time with the family when the emphasis is on fun. This is a day for all his favorites, maybe even a day at the ballpark. Whatever you plan, just make sure Dad knows he's the guest of honor!

As much as dads appreciate ties and shirts, what they really enjoy is family time with the emphasis on fun.

Let's Talk

Do you think it's harder to be a mom or a dad? Why?

What is your father's greatest strength? Why do you think so?

What is your father's least favorite activity?

Which television fathers are the most realistic?

What's your favorite memory of time spent with your dad?

Do you have friends who have difficult relationships with their fathers?
How does that affect their relationship with God?

How do you think Jesus might have celebrated Father's Day with Saint Joseph?

Let's Listen

Genesis 37   Exodus 20:12   Proverbs 17:5–7   Luke 15

Let's Cook

RIB-EYE STEAKS WITH SWEETENED BLUE CHEESE CILANTRO BUTTER, FRESH SPINACH IN WARM BACON DRESSING

Pull out the old recipes for those dishes like Mom used to make, or surprise Dad with a menu that's just for him. No dainty tea sandwiches here!

Chill the sweet blue cheese cilantro butter in a fancy mold to create a decoration for the steaks!

Rib-Eye Steaks with Sweetened Blue Cheese Cilantro Butter
Serves: 4 | Prep Time: 60 Minutes (including marinade) | Cooking Time: 15 Minutes

4 rib-eye steaks
2 teaspoons salt
1 teaspoon black pepper
1 teaspoon garlic powder
4 teaspoons olive oil
4 teaspoons Worcestershire sauce
2 teaspoons green peppercorns (optional)

BLUE CHEESE CILANTRO BUTTER
½ cup crumbled blue cheese
4 teaspoons fresh cilantro, finely chopped
4 tablespoons butter
2 teaspoons honey

1 lemon, cut into 4 wedges (for garnish)

Prepare grill or turn oven to broil. Season rib-eyes with salt, pepper, garlic powder, olive oil, and Worcestershire sauce and marinate for about 1 hour.

Optional: Crush green peppercorns by putting in a plastic bag and pressing with a flat frying pan. Remove peppercorns from bag and distribute over the steaks, pressing the crushed peppercorns into the meat.

In a separate bowl, add the blue cheese, cilantro, butter, and honey and mix together. If necessary, heat for 30 seconds in the microwave to help the melting and mixing process. Set aside in refrigerator until ready to serve.

To cook steaks, place rib-eyes directly on the heat for 5 to 7 minutes on each side for medium-rare steaks. After the steaks are cooked, scoop a teaspoon of the sweetened blue cheese butter to melt over the hot steaks. Serve with a lemon wedge to add another level of fresh flavor.

Tradition tells us that Saint Joseph is also called the Universal Protector of the Church because of his role in safeguarding Jesus and Mary from Herod's plan.

Fresh Spinach in Warm Bacon Dressing

Serves: 4 | Prep Time: 10 Minutes | Cooking Time: 5 Minutes

8 strips thick-cut bacon
3 teaspoons strawberry jam
3 teaspoons cider vinegar
3 teaspoons mustard
¼ teaspoon black pepper
8 cups fresh baby spinach leaves (2 bags prewashed spinach)

Cut bacon into ¼-inch strips. Cook in a pan until crispy and place to the side. Remove pan from heat and drain three-quarters of the bacon grease. With the remaining bacon grease still in the pan, add strawberry jam, vinegar, mustard, and black pepper and stir together. Return pan to heat and add spinach. Toss everything in the pan until spinach begins to wilt. Remove from heat immediately and sprinkle with crumbled pieces of bacon. Serve warm.

CHAPTER 12

Be Mine

SUGGESTED FOR THE FEAST OF THE SACRED HEART OF JESUS

. . . that Christ may dwell in your hearts through faith; that you, rooted and

grounded in love, may have strength to comprehend with all the holy ones what

is the breadth and length and height and depth, and to know the

love of Christ that surpasses knowledge . . .

EPHESIANS 3:17–19A

The Bible teaches that believers are new creations in Christ and that our regeneration extends all the way to our cores—to our hearts. What an awesome thought! Jesus' love for those who come to Him in faith is so complete that He offers His heart as a replacement for their cold and stony one. It's a total transplant, one that cuts away the blockages caused by old hurts and the disease of sin and unbelief. When we trust in Christ, He puts His heart in us so we can love like Him and learn to live like Him!

The enormity of this gift and its implications is so radical we are tempted to dismiss it as impossible. The enemy of our souls comes to accuse us and remind us of all our failures. When we give in to Satan's schemes instead of trusting God's promises, we revert to our old habits of relying on our flawed feelings and judgment. We remain pressed down by old guilt. Our lives are cold and empty unless we take the time to measure our version of love against God's.

Even if we work hard at trying to be kind, even if we think we are loving compared to other people, we can't get beyond caring on a human level. Human love gets tangled up in human concerns like reciprocity and worthiness.

The love that comes from God is entirely different from human love. The source of this love is uniquely divine rather than human and its outworking is unconditional, not dependent on any merit. Paul writes to the believers in Corinth, "Love is patient, love is kind. It is not jealous, it is not pompous, it is not inflated, it is not rude, it does not seek its own interests, it is not quick-tempered, it does not brood over injury, it does not rejoice over wrongdoing but rejoices with the truth. It bears all things, believes all things, hopes all things, endures all things. Love never fails."

Agape *is the Greek word for God's love, which is a sacrificial type of love.*

When we love with Christ's love we are able to love without concern for ourselves. We are able to love without concern for our reputations or our reward because they are protected and provided for by Christ. We love because we are loved. We forgive because Christ forgives us.

We give because Christ gives to us. Our decision to act out of love is no longer dependent on our ability to love. Instead, we consider the greatness of Christ's love toward us and how He might be honored as His love is expressed through us as we serve others.

Consider the impact of shifting perspective like this. Motivated by Christ's love, we would be able to put aside the things that distress us or make us feel uncomfortable and focus our attention on the people who need our love, whether we find them in our streets and shelters, our prisons, our hospitals, or our own homes. Expecting no more than Christ did from the people He came to die for, we would remember Him and reflect His selfless love for us. Because of His love, we can love our enemies and do good to those who hate us. How many family disagreements would be resolved in an instant if one person in the dispute decided to let Christ love through him or her, speaking and acting out of kindness instead of anger? How many people would find emotional and spiritual healing if they were able to seek God's attitude toward a person who has done them a great wrong and choose forgiveness over revenge or hatred? How many relationships would be restored if we cared more about repair and restoration than we did about demanding our "right" to restitution? How many prodigal sons and daughters are longing for the welcoming hug of a parent who loves them and wants them to have a fresh start?

These are not theoretical questions. Nothing provides a clearer picture of our faith than our life of love. We may talk all we want about our virtues, but the truth is exposed in how brightly Christ's love shines through us.

The Feast of the Sacred Heart of Jesus is celebrated on the second Friday following Pentecost. It's Jesus' Valentine's Day!

Let's Talk

How is God's love different from human love?

Who is difficult for you to love? What happens when the challenge changes from
how you can love that person to how God can love that person through you?

Who is the most loving person you know? What qualities does that person exhibit?

Sometimes teens are pressured on dates to "prove their love."
Why is such a request proof that the person making it is not exhibiting love?

Jesus showed love to the outcasts of His time on earth.
In your community, who are considered the outcasts, and how might you show them God's love?

In the next twenty-four hours, what three things could you do to
share God's love in your neighborhood?

Let's Listen

I Corinthians 13   Galatians 4:6   Colossians 3:15–17

I Thessalonians 3:11–13   I Peter 3:15

Let's Cook

OSSO BUCCO
GARLIC WHIPPED MASHED POTATOES

Who would Jesus feed today? This is an opportunity to exhibit love by preparing a meal for someone who would not expect it or for someone who is a stranger in your community, like an international student. Perhaps you and your family could be a part of preparing and serving a meal for many by volunteering at a community shelter, your local "Meals on Wheels," or a similar community outreach program. This menu offers a special meal—from the heart!

Osso Bucco
BRAISED VEAL SHANKS

Serves: 4 | Prep Time: 25 Minutes | Cooking Time: 2 Hours

4 veal shanks
2 teaspoons salt
1 teaspoon black pepper
½ cup flour
4 tablespoons olive oil
2 garlic cloves, minced
1 small onion, finely minced
2 celery stalks, chopped into ¼-inch pieces
2 carrots, chopped into ¼-inch pieces
2 cups dry white wine
1 cup beef broth
4 tablespoons tomato paste
2 bay leaves

Preheat oven to 275 degrees. When preparing the shanks, leave the bone in the center. Season the shanks with salt and pepper and dredge in flour. Shake off extra flour. Add olive oil to a hot pan and carefully sear the shanks, cooking 2 to 4 minutes on each side or until shanks are a brown caramelized color. Remove shanks and place in a deep baking dish. Set aside.

To the hot pan, add garlic, onion, celery, and carrots. Let cook in the oil for 2 to 3 minutes. Add wine, beef broth, and tomato paste. Use whisk to mix drippings from the bottom of the pan. Add bay leaves and let simmer for 2 to 3 minutes, allowing alcohol to cook out. Add 2 to 3 pinches of salt and pepper to taste.

Pour the wine-and-broth mixture over the shanks and cover with foil. Use a fork to poke some holes in the foil to allow steam to be released. Cook in the oven for 1½ to 2 hours or until the meat falls off the bone.

Garlic Whipped Mashed Potatoes

Serves: 4 | Prep Time: 10 Minutes | Cooking Time: 25 Minutes

1 quart water
4 large potatoes
4 tablespoons butter
2 garlic cloves, minced
½ cup heavy whipping cream
2 teaspoons salt
½ teaspoon pepper
3 to 4 teaspoons fresh parsley, minced

Boil water in a large pot. Peel and cut potatoes in quarters and add to boiling water. Cook for approximately 20 to 25 minutes or until potatoes are fork tender. Ladle out 1 cup of starchy water and save. Drain the rest of the water and keep potatoes in pot. Using a potato masher, begin to mash the potatoes.

In a separate microwave-safe bowl, melt butter, garlic, heavy whipping cream, salt, pepper, and parsley together and cook for about 1 minute. Add this garlic butter to the potatoes and continue to mash or whip with a hand blender. Add saved starchy potato water as needed for desired consistency.

When you show love by feeding the hungry, you offer far more than just a meal.

CHAPTER 13

Living in Liberty

For you were called for freedom, brothers. But do not use this freedom as an

opportunity for the flesh; rather, serve one another through love. For the whole law

is fulfilled in one statement, namely, "You shall love your neighbor as yourself."

GALATIANS 5:13—14

As the Constitutional Congress closed its deliberations in 1787, one of the anxious observers outside of the hall asked Benjamin Franklin, "Well, Doctor, what have we got—a monarchy or a republic?" Franklin replied, "A republic, if you can keep it." Our founders, especially the wise elder statesmen like Franklin, knew the government they were establishing for the United States of America was an experiment. Its success depended more on the commitment of its citizens than the skill of its designers. If the citizens could trust the leaders they chose and hold them to a standard of excellence as they performed their duties, the experiment would be a model for the rest of the world. If the citizens abdicated their responsibilities and ceded all the authority to those in power, the experiment would be a failure.

While our record is not perfect, our experimental republic is well into its third century. Our form of government has been replicated in other nations that have gained their freedom. And it remains the model for those who believe that the biblical principle of servant leadership is the ideal for those who govern.

This principle is so important to us it has been embedded in our American idioms. The term we use for government work in the United States is "public service." That term denotes our expectation that those who obtain elective office or accept appointments in our government take up their positions with the intent to uphold the law and serve others fairly and honorably, even when that service comes at a personal cost to them. We will not tolerate unethical behavior in any official, even if that conduct can be defended as meeting the letter of the law.

The biblical principle of servant leadership should be the ideal for those who govern.

Citizens uphold their end of the contract by following the law, being informed about issues and candidates, and casting their votes for those whom they believe most capable and most fit for the responsibility of office. Citizens also bear a responsibility to make sure the promises made in a political campaign are actually kept. This is not easy work, but it is not impossible. A call or an e-mail is all it takes to make your opinion heard. The people who are most effective in office are those who want to know what their constituents think about the decisions they're making in committees and open sessions.

Parents often tell their children that only in America can any child grow up to be president. That's a tradition we can protect by encouraging any child with an interest in government to pursue that high goal. But America also needs service-minded people who will take some time from their full-time careers to be school board members, county commissioners, mayors, and town council representatives. If the official biographies on the United States Senate and

*Let's remember
that freedom is a
gift that should
never be abused.
Freedom is
not cheap!*

House of Representatives websites are a good indicator, these local offices can also be great places from which to launch a career in Congress, or even in the White House.

One of the luxuries of liberty is the freedom to be critical. In this country, late-night comedians fill their monologues with jokes about the people in power. The most successful politicians learn to take the jabs with a smile. One famous United States senator collected thirty years' worth of political cartoons that took aim at him and covered the walls of his office with the best of them. Every year, the president is the guest of honor at dinners hosted by the National Press Club and the White House Correspondents, getting his share of laughs by turning the tables on the people who make their living finding fault with him. This give-and-take is an American tradition that exemplifies the strength of our democracy.

All of our American freedoms—the right to vote, the right to worship openly, an independent press—are genuine blessings. We pass them from one generation to the next by taking care to assure the strength of our democracy and by showing our children that we value the privilege of liberty. Many of our parents and grandparents crossed oceans, often risking their lives, so their children could have better lives in America. When we celebrate our country, we honor our founders and our families for the heritage they gave us: life in the land of the free and the home of the brave.

Let's Talk

Which American freedom would you most hate to lose? Why?

Which freedom would you be willing to give up in exchange for something else?

Have you ever read the words to the national anthem? Do you know its background story?

*If you were asked to nominate a different song to be our national anthem,
what would you pick? Why?*

*Do you know someone who came to America to escape political tyranny?
Have you ever asked about his or her experiences?*

*What is your favorite Fourth of July family tradition?
What is a tradition you'd like to add to your celebration?*

*Have you ever attended a government session or meeting?
Have you ever thought about running for office? Which one?*

Let's Listen

Psalm 119:44–46   Isaiah 61   Luke 4:14–21   Galatians 5

Let's Cook

ITALIAN SAUSAGES WITH ORANGES, CILANTRO, BLUE CHEESE, AND BARBECUE SAUCE
RAMEN SALAD WITH GRILLED CORN AND SCALLIONS

Freedom is not just about government, it's also personal. This is a good day to encourage those who are trying to free themselves from bad habits that have taken away their freedom. Expand your guest list to include someone who will appreciate your hospitality and your support.

This easy-to-make recipe isn't always so easy to eat. But as with Sloppy Joes, the messiness is worth it!

Italian Sausages with Oranges, Cilantro, Blue Cheese, and Barbecue Sauce

Serves: 6 | Prep Time: 15 Minutes | Cooking Time: 40 Minutes

12 Italian sausages (sweet or hot)
3 teaspoons olive oil
Juice of 1 orange (approximately
   2 to 3 tablespoons)
1 teaspoon orange zest
¼ teaspoon red pepper flakes
½ cup blue cheese (cheddar cheese may be
   substituted)
½ cup barbecue sauce
12 hot dog buns

Preheat oven to 375 degrees. Prepare sausages by cutting a ¼-inch slit lengthwise to create a "pocket" to stuff. Place sausages on a baking pan, allowing at least ½-inch separation between them.

In a separate bowl, mix the olive oil, orange juice, orange zest, red pepper flakes, cheese, and barbecue sauce. Mix thoroughly. Using a teaspoon, insert some of the barbecue-and-cheese mix into the split sausages. Bake sausages for 25 to 30 minutes and serve on hot dog buns for easy eating.

Ramen Salad with Grilled Corn and Scallions

Serves: 6 | Prep Time: 25 Minutes | Cooking Time: 10 Minutes

2 ears corn on the cob
2 packs ramen noodles (do not use the spice packet)
8 cups shredded iceberg lettuce
2 scallion stems, minced
2 carrots, shredded
4 teaspoons soy sauce
4 tablespoons olive oil
4 tablespoons white or apple cider vinegar
½ teaspoon salt
¼ teaspoon pepper

Fire up grill to high heat. Clean and prepare corn by pulling back the husk, but leave it attached to the cob. Remove the corn silk and discard. After the corn is cleaned, return the leaves to cover the cob and soak the whole corn on the cob in water for about 10 minutes. Place the whole corn on the grill for approximately 10 to 15 minutes, turning every 2 to 3 minutes. The water from the soaking will steam the corn, while the grilled leaves will add a smoky flavor to it. Once it's cooked, let corn cool before shaving off the kernels into a bowl.

Prepare rest of salad by breaking up the ramen noodles in the bowl of corn. Add all of the other ingredients and mix well, so that the noodles begin to soak up the liquids. Let the salad sit in the liquids for at least 10 minutes before adding salt and pepper to taste.

America,
America,
God shed His
grace on thee!

CHAPTER 14

Generation to Generation

Great is the LORD and worthy of high praise; God's grandeur is beyond understanding.

One generation praises your deeds to the next and proclaims your mighty works.

They speak of the splendor of your majestic glory, tell of your wonderful deeds.

PSALM 145:3—5

In our society, grandparents often occupy a very different position than they do in other parts of the world, and that is a great loss. Instead of being our close neighbors, grandparents can live thousands of miles away. Leisurely daily contact has given way to weekly phone calls and event-packed visits during which most of the time is taken up in the exchange of highlights and data. The end result can be families who know a lot of facts about each other, but do not actually know each other.

Grandparents are supposed to play an important role in the lives of their grandchildren, but not the one often seen. It is not the grandparents' place to impose their opinions on family management or child discipline. Nor is it their right to exert influence or use bribes to convince their grandchildren to follow their directives when the decision should be the parents'. Grandparents are called to a much higher responsibility.

It is the privilege of grandparents to offer perspective. They have not earned their experience so they can be managers, but so they can be encouragers. When parents are unsure they can manage the task of parenthood, grandparents aren't there to argue or to rescue, but to provide a gentle reminder that along with the gift of children, God provides everything parents need to care for each child.

All those years in the stands as number one soccer mom or team dad are actually training for the big leagues, when our sons and daughters become parents themselves and need reassurance that they are doing a great job. The same rules supportive moms and dads follow with their children after every ball game apply when supporting a parent. Focus on the positive. Remind rookie parents of the things they are doing well as they learn to care for their own children. In the grand scheme of things, it makes no difference at all if grandchildren have a different sleep and meal schedule than the one that worked for their parents. Grandparents are doing their job when they ignore all those incidentals and concentrate on the sweet sound of young parents reading a classic fairy tale or praying with their little one at bedtime. Grandparents are supposed to watch from the stands and tell the new team what looks good, cheering hard, especially on the tough days.

Grandparents also have the matchless responsibility of freely loving grandchildren without being distracted by jelly smears, unmade beds, or grades. Without subverting the rules parents have established, grandparents can provide the hugs and winks that tell children they are doing okay even when they color outside the lines. Spilled milk, a broken dish, a ball through the neighbor's window, a dented fender,

> *It is the privilege of grandparents to offer perspective.*

or a missed curfew won't upset a grandparent with a good memory. That means everything to a child surrounded by frowns and the prospect of being grounded. Building a record of reliable acceptance creates channels of communication that will stay strong in the rockiest of times, including times of teen rebellion against parental authority.

Above every other responsibility and privilege that might come to grandparents is the one laid out again and again in the Bible—faith formation. Grandparents are entrusted with recounting God's goodness. They must tell the stories of grace over and over so their children and grandchildren can memorize the details and be ready to pass this history to the next generation. Grandparents know how God worked in the years before they were born, and they know their stories that must be added to the family history. Their testimony of faith and encouragement makes an impression that remains long after they are no longer alive.

Grandparents can provide the hugs and winks that tell children they are doing okay.

Finally, and most importantly, grandparents have the responsibility to pray for their grandchildren. The work of prayer is not hindered by distance or age or even infirmity. Can there be any more treasured inheritance than the knowledge that a loving grandparent never stopped praying, never stopped believing, never stopped trusting in God's faithfulness to all generations?

Carlos and Fe Patalinghug with their extended family.

Let's Talk

Do you think older people are stereotyped in our society?

Why do some kids find it easier to talk to their grandparents than to their parents?

Do you have a favorite memory or story about each of your grandparents?

What plans for life did your grandparents have at your age?
What dreams for the future do they have now?

If you could give each of your grandparents one special day,
and there were no limits on your plans, what would you do?

What do you think of as old? What are the signs of old age?

How often should grandchildren be in touch with their own grandparents?

Let's Listen

Genesis 9   Joshua 22   Psalm 33

Psalm 105   Luke 1:46–56

Let's Cook

MAHIMAHI WITH CAPER MUSTARD SAUCE
ORZO PASTA WITH BUTTER AND PEAS

If your grandparents are nearby, throw them a party with heart-healthy versions of their favorite foods or surprise them with new dishes picked out just for them. If your grandparents are far away, surprise them with a delivery of foods they'll enjoy,

My grandparents love seafood! This recipe offers a taste that's different from the way they would have had it in the Philippines.

along with the latest family pictures. If they are no longer alive, use Grandparents' Day as an opportunity to honor their memory by visiting lonely seniors who are in full-time care facilities.

Mahimahi with Caper Mustard Sauce

Serves: 6 | Prep Time: 10 Minutes | Cooking Time: 15 Minutes

MAHIMAHI
6 mahimahi fillets
½ teaspoon salt
¼ teaspoon pepper
1½ cups seasoned bread crumbs
2 eggs, beaten with 2 teaspoons water
3 tablespoons olive oil

CAPER MUSTARD SAUCE
3 teaspoons butter
1½ teaspoons mustard
1 lemon, juiced
3 teaspoons capers with juice
Salt and black pepper to taste

2 tablespoons parsley, chopped (for garnish)

Season mahimahi with salt and pepper. Dredge fillets in bread crumbs. Dip fillets in egg mixture, and then dredge in bread crumbs again.

Heat olive oil in pan, and carefully place fillets in hot oil. Cook 3 to 5 minutes on each side. Once cooked, remove and place on a serving plate.

To the same pan, add butter, mustard, lemon juice, and capers. Salt and pepper to taste. Let the butter melt, and let the flavors cook together.

Pour the sauce over the breaded mahimahi. Sprinkle the parsley over the fish for garnish and extra flavor.

Orzo Pasta with Butter and Peas

Serves: 6 | Prep Time: 15 Minutes | Cooking Time: 5 Minutes

1½ cups orzo pasta
1½ cups frozen peas
3 tablespoons butter
½ teaspoon salt
¼ teaspoon pepper
¼ teaspoon garlic powder
½ cup Parmesan cheese, grated

Boil orzo pasta in water. When pasta is almost cooked, add frozen peas to the boiling water. When pasta is cooked and peas are soft, drain the water, leaving only a few tablespoons of water in the pot. Add butter, salt, pepper, and garlic powder, and mix well to incorporate flavors. Add fresh grated Parmesan cheese, and mix together before serving.

Jesus' grandparents' names are Saints Anna and Joachim. They are Mary's parents. We celebrate their feast day on July 26.

CHAPTER 15

Only a Game

WINNING AND LOSING

(But) whatever gains I had, these I have come to consider a loss because of Christ.

More than that, I even consider everything as a loss because of the supreme good of

knowing Christ Jesus my Lord. For his sake I have accepted the loss of all things

and I consider them so much rubbish, that I may gain Christ.

PHILIPPIANS 3:7—8

Competition is a basic component of human interaction. It is a God-given gift that teaches perseverance, leadership, cooperation, graciousness, and humility.

We usually think of competition in connection with sports, but competition is a part of our family relationships and our friendships. We see it when we vie for good parking spaces and the best position at the grocery checkout, and it certainly shows up in the classroom and the office.

Our country is fueled by competition; it is an essential component of our free enterprise system—the element that pushes businesses to "try harder." Successful companies and professionals want to offer better products, service, and prices so they will be known as the best in their field. Both consumers and businesses benefit in this environment. The consumer gains from being served by someone who is always trying to improve, and the business profits from increased traffic.

Competition is the power behind invention and exploration, too. Scientists from different nations have raced to find cures for diseases, recover and convert raw materials into valuable resources, and study outer space and the depths of the ocean. Millions have benefited from these efforts.

Millions more have enjoyed the excitement and pride of supporting their favorite teams, from Little League to the pros. The United States is a late entry in soccer's World Cup series, but we try to make up for that with our efforts to win gold at the Olympics. Americans often measure Olympic success by comparing the number of medals we've won to those won by the Germans or the Russians. But we can lose sight of the real value of the games when we do that. The winners are not just the athletes who finished first, second, and third, but those who participated and did their best, no matter where they finished in the standings.

That is the philosophy of competition we need to affirm in our families. Doing your best and playing by the rules are the true marks of success in any contest. Wins and losses are just statistics. Competition is not something to avoid; it's something to embrace because it motivates us to action. We cannot and should not insulate our kids or ourselves from the risks of the arena. Instead, we have to train for genuine success.

> *True competition brings out the best, not the worst, in people.*

In the classic poem "If," Kipling offers a prescription for true success in life. He says that knowing how to handle both winning and losing is one of the keys to having all that life has to offer.

His admonition is to "treat those two imposters just the same." In other words, we should not become conceited in victory or despairing in loss. But how do we find that balance, and more importantly, how do we build it into the lives of young people?

It is a daily process of celebrating the success of good efforts, the strengths that make each person special, and the love that is guaranteed in your family. This steady buildup of the positive and the permanent provides a cushion that puts both winning and losing into context.

The hurt of a loss like missing a play on the field, not being picked for a squad, finishing second in a class election, or breaking up with a boyfriend or girlfriend takes its rightful place as an event, not a defining moment. In the minutes and days after any loss, the best messages are hugs and the acknowledgment of pain. In this "teachable moment," the most important lesson your child needs is that you are standing by to help and to encourage. There is time enough for secondary lessons that will help turn the next competition into a win.

Competition teaches lessons in preseverance, leadership, cooperation, graciousness, and humility.

Understanding real success and knowing the hurt of loss are essential to learning how to win graciously. There is nothing less attractive than gloating in victory. Winners who acknowledge the hard work of their opponent, the efforts of those who helped put them in a position to win, and the divine Providence that allowed them victory display the qualities of people worthy to be known as champions.

Let's Talk

Who do you compete with at home and at school? What do you compete over?

Who is your favorite athlete? How does he or she respond to winning and losing?

Some schools have eliminated team tryouts and let anyone who is interested join the team of his or her choice. Do you think this is a good idea? Why or why not?

How do you feel when you hear someone's parent yelling at him or her
from the stands or after a game? Why do some parents behave like that?

Is losing related to being a loser?

If you were preparing an acceptance speech for an award, what would you say?

Let's Listen

Psalm 44   Proverbs 3   Isaiah 5:8–30

Luke 9   Thessalonians 4:9–12

Let's Cook

Get your team together to celebrate good effort and lessons learned, no matter what the rankings look like. Reminisce about the fun moments and honor the unique contributions made by each team member. This is a good time to try out a casserole or pasta recipe. Serve it with a salad and let the team pitch in with their favorite appetizers and desserts.

Hearty Bolognese

Serves: 4 | Prep Time: 20 Minutes | Cooking Time: 20 Minutes

3 tablespoons olive oil
½ cup onions, chopped
½ cup celery, chopped
¼ cup carrots, chopped
2 garlic cloves, chopped
2 bay leaves (if dried, chop or grind in a
    pestle or food processor)
½ cup mushrooms, sliced (optional)
¼ pound ground beef
¼ pound ground pork
¼ pound ground veal
½ teaspoon salt
½ teaspoon pepper
2 cups white wine
½ cup heavy whipping cream
6 ounces tomato paste
1-pound box thick spaghetti
2 to 5 cups boiled pasta water, reserved
    (add according to the desired thickness
    of sauce)
¼ cup fresh Parmesan cheese, grated

Heat a large pot with olive oil. Sauté onions, celery, carrots, garlic, and bay leaves (and mushrooms, if using). Add the meats, salt, and pepper and cook thoroughly, mixing all of the ingredients together. Cook uncovered for about 10 to 15 minutes.

After meat is cooked, add wine and cream. Cook until alcohol smell dissipates, about 5 minutes. Add the tomato paste and mix thoroughly, creating a paste-like sauce.

Heat water to a boil and add pasta. When the pasta is cooked al dente, remove it from the water and place it into the sauce. Reserve 2 to 4 cups starchy water and gradually add into the sauce until it has a thick, chili-like consistency. Mix in Parmesan cheese to help thicken and flavor the sauce.

Top off each serving with a little more freshly grated Parmesan cheese and a drizzle of extra-virgin olive oil.

Garlic Bread

Serves: 4 | Prep Time: 10 Minutes | Cooking Time: 10 Minutes

2 mini baguettes
¼ cup mayonnaise
¼ teaspoon garlic powder
¼ teaspoon salt
¼ teaspoon black pepper
½ teaspoon parsley, freshly chopped

Preheat oven to 400 degrees. Cut mini baguettes in half, creating 4 equal-sized open-faced buns.

In a bowl, mix mayonnaise, garlic powder, salt, pepper, and parsley. Using a spatula, evenly spread a coating of the mixture over each piece of bread.

Put the bread on a cookie sheet, and place in oven for 8 to 10 minutes or until the mayonnaise becomes golden brown.

Left to right: me; my father, Carlos Sr.;
and my brother, Carlos Jr.;
in the early 1990s.

As a young man, I enjoyed competing in a martial art called Arnis, which is Philippine full-contact stick fighting. In 1991, I won a gold medal in my sparring division.

CHAPTER 16

You're Hired

LANDING A FIRST JOB

Then David said to his son Solomon: "Be firm and steadfast; go to work without

fear or discouragement, for the LORD God, my God, is with you.

He will not fail you or abandon you before you have completed all the work

for the service of the house of the LORD."

I CHRONICLES 28:20

It's a day parents think they long for—that day when the child who has depended on them for just about everything discovers the power of an income of his or her own.

The amount of that income doesn't matter. The significance is in the step toward independence and adulthood. It is indeed an event worth celebrating. Your child getting hired means an impartial judge has determined that he or she has valuable qualities that are in demand. Those qualities are most likely dependability, punctuality, and trustworthiness, qualities you have worked hard to instill, so it is a double cause for celebration.

Being the parent of an employee is different from being the parent of a student or a team member or a scout. There is no "parents' night" to attend, and no parent conferences where a child's boss gives a progress report, or a parent explains that an undone assignment was the result of an unexpected family outing. Aside from being alert to a situation that might be dangerous or illegal, parents have no standing with employers. They are not advocates for their child, and they are not participants in the relationship between employer and employee or employee and coworker or employee and customer.

This is not an easy transition to make. Parents are fiercely loyal. They do not like to hear that someone was displeased with their child. They want to step in when it seems their child is being treated unfairly. They worry about risks. They want to be first on their child's list of priorities. The feelings are reminiscent of the ones they had that day long ago when it was time to walk out of the kindergarten classroom and let somebody else become a major influence in that child's life.

The support and encouragement you offer your new wage earner today will lay the groundwork for the two of you to talk in the future about one of the most important areas of your child's adult life. You also are helping to shape a pattern that will persist when that child is building a career. You and your child are entering a new phase of your relationship, and your ability to listen, to offer counsel when needed, and to encourage independence are more critical than ever.

When your child tells you the boss was grouchy or the customer was rude or the work was hard, you have to say, "I'm sorry to hear that. Do you want to talk about it?" You cannot say, "How dare he!" or "I hope you told her off!" or "You don't have to do that kind of job!"

Your goal is to let your child do the work of maturing—of figuring out how to deal with grouchy bosses and rude customers and the unpleasant parts of jobs. Why? Because experience in dealing with these realities is infinitely more instructive than hearing about them from you or the world's most gifted management consultant. Cranky Mr. Smith, who is never quite satisfied with how his lawn gets cut, is good

> *Be there to listen and to remind your new wage earner of his or her ability to meet any challenge.*

106

training for cranky Dr. Smith, who rarely has a positive word for the interns he supervises. Rude customers at the drive-through window are miniature versions of rude customers with impossible demands for delivery. Knowing how to be civil in the face of incivility cannot be learned in the abstract. Handling the necessary cleanups that come along with an evening of babysitting fosters the determination and confidence to confront the more difficult aspects in every job, even the ones that seem more glamorous.

Be there to listen and to remind your child of his or her ability to meet any challenge. Express your unconditional love and your pride. Try not to act surprised when the child who was happy to spend your income on life's extras is suddenly a little more frugal with his or her income. It may be hard to imagine, but the time is not far off when you will get an invitation to dinner with your child, and you will not be allowed to pick up the tab. That, too, will be a day for celebration!

As your child enters this new phase of maturity, your support and encouragement are more critical than ever.

Let's Talk

Why do you think it's hard for some kids to find their first jobs?

What are some ways to get over those hurdles?

What kinds of first jobs were available to your parents but aren't around anymore? Why did they disappear? What kinds of part-time jobs are new to your generation? Why were they created?

If you were to create a business, what would it be? How would you find customers? What would you charge?

How would you respond to someone's criticism if you didn't think it was justified?

Do you think it's good for kids to have jobs of their own? What are some valid reasons for kids not to work outside the home?

What would you buy with your own money? What would you save for? What good cause would you give to?

Let's Listen

Genesis 2　　　Exodus 35　　　Matthew 20

John 6:25–59　　　I Thessalonians 4:11

Let's Cook

SEARED AHI TUNA STEAKS WITH WASABI MAYO
PAN-SEARED EGGPLANT

As we grow up, so should our tastes! Make this meal memorable by including something as new as the new job.

Tuna can be as simple as a sandwich or as fancy as sushi-grade ahi!

Seared Ahi Tuna Steaks with Wasabi Mayo

Serves: 4 | Prep Time: 15 Minutes | Cooking Time: 20 Minutes

SEARED AHI TUNA STEAKS
4 tuna steaks at least 1½ inches thick
2 tablespoons olive oil
¼ teaspoon salt
¼ teaspoon pepper
½ cup Italian seasoned bread crumbs

WASABI MAYO
¼ cup mayonnaise
¼ teaspoon dried wasabi mix (or 1 teaspoon
of fresh-grated horseradish)
2 pinches paprika
1 tablespoon fresh lemon juice

Season ahi tuna steaks with olive oil, salt, and pepper, then dredge in bread crumbs.

Heat a nonstick pan over high heat. Right before putting the tuna on the pan, turn down flame to medium heat in order to sear but not burn the steaks. Cook for 2 to 3 minutes on each side for a rare tuna that will have a soft red color in the middle. To make the tuna well-done, cook each steak 5 to 7 minutes on each side.

To make the wasabi mayo, add the mayonnaise, wasabi mix or freshly grated horseradish, paprika, and lemon juice to a bowl. Mix together.

Add a small dollop of the mayo to the top of each tuna steak as it is taken off the grill.

Adding the new worker's schedule to your family's calendar might make meal times a little more hectic. Crockpot dishes and cooked selections from the deli can help.

Pan-Seared Eggplant

Serves: 4 | Prep Time: 10 Minutes | Cooking Time: 20 Minutes

¼ cup olive oil
1 garlic clove, finely minced
½ large eggplant cut into ½-inch cubes
    (4 to 6 cups cubed eggplant)
2 teaspoons butter
6 tablespoons soy sauce
2 tablespoons fresh lemon juice
6 teaspoons water
½ teaspoon salt
½ teaspoon red pepper flakes
1 tablespoon fresh parsley, minced

Heat olive oil in a large frying pan, and add garlic over high heat. Drop heat to medium, and add the eggplant. Let eggplant cook for approximately 12 to 15 minutes to soak up and fry in the hot oil. Occasionally stir the eggplant around so that you eventually see a seared brown color develop on its different sides. After eggplant becomes less firm, add butter, soy sauce, lemon juice, water, salt, and red pepper flakes. Mix together, and let simmer for about 5 minutes more. Prior to serving, sprinkle with the fresh minced parsley.

CHAPTER 17

Hurt and Healing

God is our refuge and our strength, an ever-present help in distress. Thus we do not

fear, though earth be shaken and mountains quake to the depths of the sea.

PSALM 46:1—2

We all remember our child's first steps, first solo bike ride, first time on stage, first soccer match. Those successes are great highlights, but parents are better prepared for the rough teen years if they remember how they handled all the bumps, bruises, tears, and failures on the way to those picture-perfect moments. Parents will again need to put those coping skills to use as their teens master the skills of adulthood.

Just as the toddler stage helps a child get acquainted with physical capabilities like running, climbing, jumping, tumbling, and even dancing, the teen stage is when a child learns about emotions. The tears and tantrums and then total happiness kids experience in the early years will seem like scale models of the highs and lows you'll see in the years between the tenth or twelfth birthday and the nineteenth.

In the teen years, parents discover that there are no training wheels, knee pads, or helmets they can supply their children to protect them from emotional bruising. They are no longer supervisors. They must learn to be trusted counselors. Veterans of this transition will be quick to say that it is more difficult than they could have imagined. Parents of teens must learn to listen carefully, speak wisely, know when to be silent, and love unconditionally.

The bumps and bruises of the teen years come from friendships, dating relationships, rejections, self-criticism, out-of-bounds behavior, and sometimes the misdeeds of adults who have abused a teen's trust. Parents can provide "first aid" by being available and approachable.

When a child says, "Do you have a minute?" you must be willing to put aside your tasks and offer your full attention. No matter how the ensuing conversation makes you feel, you have to be willing to hear the whole story without injecting your commentary. When it is your turn to speak, you must take your time and choose your words wisely. They will be salt or salve.

> *A great way to deal with a broken heart is to humbly ask, "What can I learn from this pain?" It still hurts, but the pain has meaning and purpose for our future.*

Begin with a restatement of your love for your child, your confidence in his or her value, and your certainty that God can bring good out of the worst of situations, even this one. Ask gentle questions about how he or she is feeling. Ask if there is anything you can do, unless the situation is potentially dangerous, in which case you must immediately take charge. Reaffirm your love and support as he or she works through the problem. If you sense that a hug would be welcomed at this moment, offer one.

As hard as it will be, resist any remark that your teen might read as belittlement. Do not say things like, "That's not so bad!" or "Plenty of fish in the sea," or "What did you do to cause this?" or "I should have known you couldn't handle that." Even that last remark, which sounds like self-criticism, is really a criticism of your child, just as each of the others attack his or her decision-making ability and behavior. The time for analysis might come, but this is not that time.

Instead, ask, "What would you like to do now?" and accommodate anything reasonable. Set a time when you will talk some more, and let your child have some space to think and refocus.

Use the time before that next conversation to pray for wisdom; have confidence that God will provide what you need. With the emotional thermostat turned down, you and your teen can look calmly at the source of the hurt, consider options, and begin a plan that will lead to healing. If you recognized a scene from your own life story when your child first told you about his or her hurt, and you are ready to share it, this might be a good moment. You might end your story by saying you believe the moment will come when your child will use this hurtful experience to offer someone else comfort, because that is the kind of caring person he or she is. And that is one of the many things you admire about him or her.

Seeing your child hurt is painful—that's a fact. But seeing the purpose in suffering makes it easier to bear. Someday your child will be an adult, probably a parent, and the training

Parents can provide "first aid" for the hard experiences of the teen years by being available and approachable.

needed to handle that responsibility well occurs during the teen years. He or she is learning through experience and by example, and will be equipped to guide your grandchildren through the bumps and bruises of their lives, just as you are doing now.

Let's Talk

A line in a poem by Tennyson says, " 'Tis better to have loved and lost than never to have loved at all."

Why would somebody say that?

Can you remember a time in school when your feelings were hurt? What happened? How did you cope?

Is there someone in your class who always seems to be picked on or ignored?

Have you wondered how that person feels, or how you might help the situation?

Do you know someone who cuts him- or herself or is very thin and refuses to eat more?
Has that person ever talked to you about his or her feelings?

Sometimes a boy will say that he will kill himself if the girl he likes refuses to go out with him anymore.

What would you tell a girl in that situation to do? What would you do?

Have any of your friends ever told you that a boyfriend or even a girlfriend hit him or her?
How did you respond? Would you tell somebody else? Why or why not?

If you were your own parent, and you learned that someone had mistreated you,

how would you handle the situation? Why?

Let's Listen

Nehemiah 2   Psalm 13   Jonah 1–4   Hebrews 12

Let's Cook

The most emotional conversations can be made a little easier if there's a diversion to work on together while you talk. Using your hands to mix the stuffing for a pepper can be messy, but it can also be a fun distraction. The chopping and mixing and preparation for something out of the ordinary like fondue or shish kabobs or a main dish salad will also offer lots of time together in the kitchen.

Comfort Stuffed Peppers

Serves: 4 | Prep Time: 15 Minutes | Cooking Time: 55 Minutes

8 ounces canned tomato sauce (or 1½ cups of your favorite spaghetti sauce)
2 peppers (any color, but shape should be fit for stuffing)
1 pound ground beef
¼ cup fresh parsley, chopped
1 tablespoon salt
½ tablespoon black pepper
2 eggs
1 medium white onion, minced
1 teaspoon garlic powder
½ cup white bread, torn into pieces
¼ cup grated Parmesan cheese
½ cup milk
4 slices provolone cheese (or ½ cup mozzarella cheese)

Preheat oven to 375 degrees. Set aside 4 tablespoons of tomato sauce for the end of the cooking process.

Prepare peppers by washing, cutting in half from stem to base, and cleaning away the seeds. Set aside in baking pan. Prepare the stuffing by mixing the ground beef with parsley, salt and pepper, eggs, minced onion, garlic powder, torn white bread, Parmesan cheese, milk, and remaining tomato/spaghetti sauce.

Using your hands to mix, combine all the ingredients thoroughly. Insert about ¼ pound of ground beef mixture into each of the peppers. Place peppers back in baking pan, and cover with foil. Using a fork, poke a few holes in the foil to release steam. Place in oven. After 50 minutes, remove the peppers, and turn oven temperature to broil.

Using the tomato sauce you've set aside, spoon about 1 to 2 teaspoons over each pepper, and top off with provolone or mozzarella cheese. Return peppers to broiler for another 3 to 5 minutes or until cheese melts and browns.

Serve over top of a bed of white rice.

CHAPTER 18

Hopes and Hugs

MOVING OUT, MOVING ON

The LORD will guard you from all evil, will always guard your life.

The LORD will guard your coming and going both now and forever.

PSALMS 121:7—8

Of course you knew this moment would come. Parenting is intended to get sons and daughters ready to accept independence. The toddler you left in the church nursery; the first-grader you entrusted to a teacher; the Scout you sent off to camp; the high school senior who made you proud—that young adult is now about to take on new responsibilities for his or her own life.

The day you take your child to that new residence is as significant in your family history as the day he or she was born. Moving out can be emotionally equivalent to cutting the umbilical cord. That first moment of physical autonomy was step one on the journey to this point.

You know that the bond between parent and child is never broken, and it is entirely possible that your child will return at some point to live under your roof, but it will never be the way it was. This moving out symbolizes moving on to adulthood, and the initial changes may be dramatic.

The rules by which your child will operate from now on are the rules he or she chooses to observe. Unless your child is attending a military academy, convent, or seminary or is on a team with a strict coach, no one at college has a personal interest in how well your child handles hygiene, cleanliness, or class assignments. No one will limit his or her consumption of soda or Snickers or fries. No one will announce bedtime at a decent hour or make sure your child is awake in time for class. For a first-year student from a home where rules and responsibilities were the norm, the level of freedom can be shocking.

Take comfort in compassion, knowing the reality of these changes is as unsettling for your child as the thought of them is for you. Parents and children both shed tears during the breaking-in period schools call orientation. Well-run schools wisely require a first-semester class that covers time management and study skills, even interpersonal skills for managing roommate relationships, to smooth the adjustment process.

Wise parents welcome every phone call, listen intently, and practice their new role as consultant rather than manager by gently and positively reminding their child that he or she is living out a dream. Tell your child you know that he or she has everything necessary to succeed and you're confident about that because you pray daily.

You might offer advice, but you must remind your child—and yourself—that the choices are his or hers, as are the consequences.

New levels of freedom can be shocking to first year students.

Professionals in higher education are concerned about a trend in over-involved parenting. Too many parents are entangling themselves in their students' lives with countless calls and text messages. Their phone calls to administrators and professors and long-distance assistance with assignments and term papers rob their children of the opportunity to fully develop into the people they could become.

Perpetual adolescents never learn the important lessons of trying and failing. They never discover the range of gifts that God has given them, or test the possible options He may have for their lives beyond what is familiar to the family. They are reluctant to leave the comfortable nest, and their parents are content to let them stay. Parents who really want to get the full value of their investment in a child's college education will step back and let their child do the work of handling adult challenges. Allow your child the joy of doing well on his or her own. If you loosen your hold, your child can begin to manage life as an independent adult, and you can enjoy your new role as trusted advisor and confidant.

You need not fear that you will be forgotten or become irrelevant. As your child moves through life, all the lessons you taught and the love you gave will become more precious. You will hear yourself quoted, and if you watch closely you will see yourself modeled someday if your child is called to become a parent.

So let your child know that you will miss him or her, but also that you are excited to see what the future holds for both of you. Tell your child you are sure that no matter how geographically far apart your family may be, God will be with each of you, binding you together as you stay close to Him.

If you loosen your hold, your college student can begin to manage life as an independent adult, and you can enjoy your new role as a trusted advisor and confidant.

Let's Talk

What do you expect to miss most about living at home with your parents when you move out on your own?

What are you looking forward to? How are you planning to stay connected to your family?

If you plan to attend college, what kind of school do you think you'd like best?

Have you talked to students or professors who teach subjects you might like to study?

Have you discussed plans to finance your higher education and learned about the kinds of aid for which you might be eligible?

What would you want your roommate to be like?

What would be impossible for you to tolerate?

Some students "crash and burn" in college by making bad decisions.

What strategies can you rely on to help you reach your goals?

Many schools offer international study options. Is there a place you would like to explore?

What do you want to learn there?

Let's Listen

Genesis 37:41–44   Jonah 1–4   Luke 3   II Timothy 4

Let's Cook

There will be plenty of time for that fall-back student diet of cheese crackers, ramen noodles, and cold pizza. Make this meal all about home-cooked favorites that are good enough to brag about. While you're getting the ingredients together, think of some other simple and nutritious meals that will keep a hardworking student in shape for those late-night study sessions.

Hearty Beef Steak Stew

Serves: 2 | Prep Time: 20 Minutes | Cooking Time: 25 Minutes

6 to 8 ounces steak (either New York strip or rib-eye), cut in ½-inch cubes
½ teaspoon salt
¼ teaspoon pepper
3 tablespoons all-purpose flour
2 tablespoons vegetable oil
1 garlic clove, minced
2 tablespoons butter
5 to 7 cups beef or vegetable stock (or 5 to 7 cups of hot water with 2 beef bouillon cubes)
2 celery stalks, cut ½ inch thick
3 carrots, cut into ½-inch sections
4 medium-sized red potatoes, cut into ¼-inch cubes
2 green peppers, cut into ¼-inch pieces
1 medium onion, cut into 4 equal sections

Add meat, salt, pepper, and flour to a large plastic bag. Seal and shake together.

In a pot or large saucepan, heat oil on high heat. Add garlic until lightly brown. Shake off the flour from the meat, and then add the meat to the hot oil and sear 1 or 2 minutes on each side. Once the meat is seared, remove and set aside.

In the same pan, add the butter to the oil. When melted, create a roux by adding the rest of the dredging flour to the butter and oil, stirring together to create a paste. Add stock, one cup at a time, constantly stirring or whisking to create a smooth texture. Once incorporated, add the rest of the liquid, and turn the heat to medium. Add the meat and the rest of the vegetables. Let simmer uncovered until the potatoes are fork tender (approximately 20 minutes). Salt and pepper to taste.

Variations

For a thicker stew, add less of the liquid (stock or water). For a soupier mix, add more water or stock, and also salt and pepper. To make a beef and noodle dish, add the noodles from one pack of ramen soup mix to the stew (do not use the flavor pouch); the noodles require only 2 to 4 minutes to cook fully. Serve with some crusty bread for a satisfying meal!

CHAPTER 19

Priceless

You formed my inmost being; you knit me in my mother's womb. I praise you,

so wonderfully you made me; wonderful are your works! . . . when I was being made

in secret, fashioned as in the depths of the earth. Your eyes foresaw my actions;

in your book all are written down; my days were shaped, before one came to be.

PSALM 139:13–16

Have you seen the *National Geographic* documentary that traces the growth of a human baby inside its mother's womb from the moment of conception to that moment when it is time to see mom's face? It's a remarkable example of science catching up with Scripture to affirm what David knew by faith and celebrated over and over again in his psalms. We are not accidents. We're not even products of an impartial assembly line. We're handmade by God Himself. And, if that weren't enough, each of us is "fearfully and wonderfully" made, intricately woven according to God's plan for us. In his letter to the church in Ephesus, the Apostle Paul added that there was nothing last-minute about that plan; we were chosen for life before the foundation of the world. Paul goes on to remind us that the absolute proof of our worth is found in the work of Christ on our behalf. We really are priceless.

Knowing what we know, we can confidently draw some important conclusions about people of every age and condition. We're not disposable, and we're not burdens. We're here on purpose and for a purpose. We are meant to value life as much as we are valued.

Every child is a blessing from God. Every parent is entrusted with the responsibility to model God's love by protecting his or her baby's life from the moment its presence is known. This is not always easy. In fact, it can seem impossible, even under the best circumstances. But God has amazing resources for parents so they can discover the blessing He intends for them as they care for the children He places in their lives.

Because of God's perfect plan, no child can truly be called "unwanted" and no pregnancy "unexpected." Could the Giver of the Law create a child who could be labeled illegitimate? Of course not! Is a child made in the image of God, our Creator and heavenly Father, ever really fatherless? No! We are not meant to be orphans, but heirs with Christ. We do not have to beg for scraps; there's a place with our name card already set at His table.

How might this knowledge shape our actions?

- It can give us confidence in God's wisdom when He instructs all of us to keep sexual relations inside marriage so we can be free to enjoy His blessings, including children, without the burdens that result from settling for less than His best for us.
- It can make us pro-life in a very practical way: We can decide that for our families, abortion is not a solution to a pregnancy.
- It can shape us as neighbors who welcome other children and their parents to our activities so they can see how God's love is expressed through families.
- It can turn us into activists who support the work of homes that offer counsel and shelter to young women who have chosen to either self-parent or release their child to adoptive parents.

> *We are not accidents. Each of us is fearfully and wonderfully made, intricately woven according to God's plan for us.*

The first Sunday in October is Respect for Life Sunday. It's a time to remember life at all stages, from conception to natural death. Life is a gift from God.

It is truly amazing that the very basic gift we all have is life! Unfortunately the label "pro-life" has become politicized, and those who call themselves pro-life are often accused of being anti-choice. Honesty before the One who gives us life raises an important question: Do we truly recognize that our life is a gift from God? If the answer is "yes," there is no other choice than to be pro-life!

Let's Talk

Have you ever thought of yourself as priceless? How might that change your opinion of yourself?

Do you wonder what God might have been thinking when He picked out your hair or decided on your height?

Are other people really priceless?

If that's true, how might that affect the way we talk about them or treat them?

How do you think your parents would respond if you announced that you were pregnant or had gotten someone pregnant? How would you want them to respond?

Have you ever thought of God's instruction that sex be reserved for marriage as one of the ways He protects you?

What do you think is the hardest part about parenting when Mom or Dad are away from home? How could you help somebody in that situation?

Let's Listen

Psalm 139   Ephesians 1   Job 38–42   Romans 8:18–39

Let's Cook

HEARTY FOUR-LAYER LASAGNA

For families with new babies, life is a blur of diapers and sleepless nights. Your unexpected gift of a real home-cooked meal would mean more than they can tell you. Make sure you've packed everything in containers that don't need to be rinsed and returned, or offer to come back later and do the dishes!

Hearty Four-Layer Lasagna

Serves: 6 | Prep Time: 40 Minutes | Cooking Time: 90 Minutes

LAYER 1
1 tablespoon olive oil
1 medium onion, minced
1 pound ground beef
½ teaspoon salt
¼ teaspoon pepper
½ teaspoon garlic powder
2 cups spaghetti sauce

To prepare the first layer, heat pan with olive oil, and sauté onions. Add ground beef, and cook uncovered for about 10 minutes over medium-high heat, stirring until brown. Add the rest of the layer 1 ingredients, and let cook for about 5 minutes. Set aside until ready to assemble.

LAYER 2
½ tablespoon butter
1 zucchini, chopped into ¼-inch cubes
1 cup sour cream
1 cup ricotta cheese
¼ cup bread crumbs
1 teaspoon salt
½ teaspoon pepper

For the second layer, in a separate pan, melt butter, add zucchini, and sauté until it becomes flexible. Do not cook fully through. Remove from heat, and place in a bowl. In the same pan, add sour cream, ricotta cheese, bread crumbs, salt, and pepper. Mix thoroughly. Set aside until ready to assemble.

LAYER 3
1 tablespoon olive oil
2 garlic cloves, minced
½ teaspoon salt
¼ teaspoon pepper
¼ teaspoon red pepper flakes
1 box frozen spinach, thawed and drained of excess water

For the third layer, in a separate pan, heat oil and sauté garlic, adding salt, pepper, and red pepper flakes. Add the thawed and drained spinach, and sauté all together. Set aside until ready to assemble.

[recipe continues on next page]

LAYER 4
¼ cup grated Parmesan cheese
¼ cup blue cheese
¼ cup shredded provolone cheese
¼ cup heavy whipping cream
2 cups spaghetti sauce

20 to 25 lasagna noodles
Butter, for the pan
1 cup shredded mozzarella cheese

To prepare layer 4, combine Parmesan cheese, blue cheese, provolone, whipping cream, and spaghetti sauce. Set aside until ready to assemble.

Use your choice of lasagna noodle (approximately 3 to 5 noodles per layer) and prepare according to instructions. Some lasagna noodles are ready to use, no boiling needed.

Lightly butter the bottom and sides of a 12-inch baking dish. When assembling the lasagna, pack in all of the various layers so the noodles and filling touch the sides of the pan. This will help keep the structure of each piece when cut.

Add one layer of lasagna noodles. Top and spread with the layer 1 meat sauce. Add another layer of lasagna, and top off with an even spread of the layer 2 ricotta-zucchini mixture. Add another layer of lasagna, and add the layer 3 spinach mix. Add the final layer of lasagna noodles, and top off with the layer 4 cheese combination. This could be refrigerated until ready to bake.

When ready to cook, cover lasagna with foil, and bake in a preheated 375 degree oven for approximately 1 hour to 1 hour 15 minutes. Remove the lasagna from the oven. Remove the foil, and add the mozzarella cheese. Return to oven for another 10 to 15 minutes or until cheese is melted and bubbling. Wait 10 to 15 minutes before cutting and serving.

CHAPTER 20

Seeking Good

SUGGESTED FOR ALL HALLOWS' EVE—OCTOBER 31

In the morning sow your seed, and at evening let not your hand be idle:

For you know not which of the two will be successful,

or whether both alike will turn out well.

ECCLESIASTES 11:6

Just when you thought it was time for families like yours to give up on Halloween, with its increasing emphasis on horror movies and mischief, God puts a verse like this where it can't be missed. The assignment from the wise author of Ecclesiastes is to do good in the evening, too, and if ever there was an evening that needs the positive influence of God's people, it's Halloween!

In the eighth century, Pope Gregory IV declared that All Saints' Day would be observed on November 1. The night before this holy or "hallowed" day was designated All Hallows' Eve, a time to prepare for the commemoration of

God's work in transforming ordinary people into extraordinary examples of faith. Halloween can still be used for that good purpose if we remember that it was originally a holy day, not a scary one!

A teen-organized party for a local church, a neighborhood, or your extended family could introduce young children to real superheroes, such as the saints or servant-styled world leaders. With a parent offering behind-the-scenes assistance if it's needed, teens can provide an evening of games and fun that will be as enjoyable for the hosts as for the kids they invite.

The satisfaction of creating the kind of event that will leave their young guests with happy memories will give teens a sense of their place and value in the bigger community.

Nobody understands the tug-of-war over Halloween better than our children, especially our teens. They're the target audience for dark films and video games that devalue life. Whereas Halloween was once a day when neighborhood kids could walk freely, it has become a day when "black magic" and the dark cults seem to have

> *All Hallows' Eve was created as a time to prepare for the commemoration of God's work in transforming ordinary people into extraordinary examples of faith.*

their greatest audience. Although we can't avoid children's desire to go trick-or-treating, we can encourage older children to see a deeper meaning in the day and the season.

A party (planned for the early part of the day if children trick-or-treat or on the weekend closest to Halloween) can provide teens with a chance to have fun, be with friends, and experience a deeper meaning of this celebration. Here's the twist: Teens plan the party not for themselves, but for younger siblings who are still too young to be exposed to the ugly scenarios that make Halloween less than hallowed.

Give teens an opportunity to be servants. Offer them a chance to exercise some responsibility rather than pull pranks. They're perfect for the job! Teens are young enough to know what younger kids will enjoy and what will bore them. Plus, they have the creativity to come up with the entertainment and the energy to keep up with the youngest guests. Teens will enjoy showing novices how to bob for apples or whistle with a mouthful of crackers. The messy process of making popcorn balls or caramel apples won't bother them. And when coaching relay teams or leading a scavenger hunt, they'll have as much fun as their guests.

If your teens ask for ideas, suggest that they have their elementary-age guests come dressed as a Bible character or a hero from church history. Younger guests will enjoy dressing up as part of God's creation—animal, vegetable, or even mineral! Suggest that they offer prizes for the most original costume or the best story about the character selected. Be sure to take lots of pictures and make them available to the grateful parents.

Enjoy the party and the satisfaction of giving the holiday back to the kids by overcoming evil with good. Praise your proactive teens for becoming heroes themselves! Imagine what a great compliment it would be if a younger brother or sister decided to dress up not like a goblin or a clown, but like his or her new hero—an older brother or sister!

The spiritual meaning of Halloween can get lost in the costumes and candy. Remind children why we celebrate with a discussion at a family meal before you go trick-or-treating!

Let's Talk

Why do you think there's a market for horror movies? How did they get so connected to Halloween?

Some people keep their children from participating in Halloween activities because they are concerned for the children's safety. What are the pluses and minuses of that decision?

Who would you pick if you were going to dress up as a figure from the Bible or Church history? What part of their story is most interesting to you?

Have you ever asked your parents about the ways their families celebrated Halloween when they were younger? What are their most vivid memories?

Do you know teens who are heavily involved in violent computer games? How does this hobby affect them? Why do the games seem so addictive?

When you become a parent, what rules will you have about watching movies or playing computer games? How will you handle the reality that your rules might be different from those of your child's friends?

Let's Listen

Wisdom 3:1–9   Ezekiel 37:1–14   Luke 24:36–43   Revelations 21:1–8

Let's Cook

PUMPKIN AND RICOTTA "WONTON-OLIS" WITH SAGE BUTTER SAUCE

When selecting foods for your kid-friendly party, incorporate healthy choices like fresh fall fruit along with the candy. Make sure the hosts will have enough energy to keep up with their guests by

Pumpkin mix can also be used for savory foods, not just for sweet pies.

preparing a pre-party meal for them that takes advantage of the fall's best foods.

Pumpkin and Ricotta "Wonton-olis" with Sage Butter Sauce
Serves: 4 | Prep Time: 30 Minutes | Cooking Time: 20 Minutes

WONTON-OLIS
1 cup ricotta cheese, strained
1 egg
¼ teaspoon nutmeg
1 cup canned pumpkin pie mix
1 teaspoon salt
½ teaspoon pepper
40 wonton wrappers

Prepare the ravioli filling by combining ricotta cheese, egg, nutmeg, pumpkin pie mix, salt, and pepper. Mix until all the ingredients are well incorporated.

Assemble the ravioli by separating the wonton wrappers on a tray lined with parchment or wax paper. Place ¾ teaspoon of the mixture in the center of each wonton wrapper. Dip your finger in warm water and moisten the exposed wonton around the pumpkin filling. Flip one end of the wonton wrapper over to enclose the pumpkin mixture, gently pressing on the sides to seal it. Be careful to avoid air bubbles. The end result should look like small triangles with the pumpkin stuffing. Repeat this process until there are about 10 wonton-olis per person.

Place wonton-olis uncovered in refrigerator and let dry (or freeze for later use).

[recipe continues on next page]

SAGE BUTTER SAUCE
4 tablespoons salted butter
8 fresh sage leaves
½ teaspoon salt
¼ teaspoon pepper
½ to 1 cup warm starchy water (from the boiling ravioli)

½ cup fresh Parmesan cheese, grated
1 loaf Italian bread

When ready to cook, boil a large pot of salted water and add the pumpkin-stuffed wontons. Be sure not to overcrowd the pot. This generally means cooking 12 to 15 wontons at a time, depending on size of the pot. Let cook for approximately 5 to 7 minutes or until you see the wonton-olis start to float in the boiling water. Scoop them out and set aside. Reserve at least ½ cup of the starchy water for the sauce. (You may also deep-fry the wontons instead of boiling them; see note below.)

Prepare the sage butter sauce by melting the butter in a large frying pan. Add the fresh sage leaves and salt and pepper. Add ½ cup of starchy pasta water to help thicken the sauce.

Add the wonton-olis to the sage butter sauce and sauté for 2 to 4 minutes. Add Parmesan cheese and let melt. The sauce should thicken slightly but still remain somewhat soupy. Serve with crusty bread to help "mop up" the sauce!

For Deep-Fried Wonton-olis
Heat 1 cup of vegetable oil over medium heat in a deep frying pan. Carefully add wonton-olis to the hot oil, making sure not to overcrowd the pan. Cook approximately 3 to 5 minutes per side. When both sides are brown, remove and place on paper towels to absorb excess grease. Sprinkle with salt immediately. Serve with your favorite dipping sauce (cheese, tomato, or sweet-and-sour work well).

CHAPTER 21

New Creations

SUGGESTED FOR ALL SAINTS' DAY

For by grace you have been saved through faith, and this is not from you; it is the

gift of God; it is not from works, so no one may boast. For we are his handiwork,

created in Christ Jesus for the good works that God has prepared in advance,

that we should live in them.

EPHESIANS 2:8—10

"Amazing Grace, how sweet the sound that saved a wretch like me." Millions have sung those familiar words since John Newton wrote them in the 1700s. According to his own writings and the accounts of the day, Newton wasn't taking poetic license when he used the word "wretch" to describe himself. Before he was transformed by grace, he was famously profane, self-absorbed, cynical about spiritual things, and in pursuit of what was often called "riotous living." Newton had disappointed his father, abused his friends, and wasted his talents. If his mother had still been alive when Newton was a young adult, she would have wept. She was a believer, and her last moments with her seven-year-old son were spent in prayer for him to live a life of faith. But as he grew into his teens, he went in the exact opposite direction. John Newton was indeed a wretch, not unlike any of us who once walked our own paths away from the Savior.

The truth about God's love for us is that He knows our sinful nature apart from His transforming grace. He saw our helplessness and hopelessness and provided for our needs even when we were unable to ask. The Apostle John sums it up this way: "For God so loved the world that He gave His only Son, so that everyone who believes in Him might not perish but might have eternal life." By His life and sacrifice and resurrection, Jesus gives us life. It is a gift of grace, which is defined as unmerited favor.

When we believe, God gives us new life. We are no longer captive to sin. We are now counted among the saints.

That idea might amuse you at first because we use the word "saint" to refer to people who are exemplary models for the rest of us. Those people have been honored by the Church and presented as ideal heroes of the faith.

We have a hard time picturing ourselves in the same grouping, but in fact, when we are transformed by grace, we too become saints in the making. We become people who are willing to follow Christ and willing to live in obedience to His commands. We are changed, like John Newton and Saints Francis, Paul, and Augustine were changed, from being eager to follow our own whims, to being eager to do what pleases our Savior. To evoke the Biblical image, when we are grafted onto the tree of life, we want to bear good fruit and plenty of it. As we mature in faith, we move from assuming we could never live like a favorite saint, to examining that saint's life and resolving to change so that we might better reflect Christ.

We live in a special time: The Church is considering the elevation of Blessed Mother Teresa of Calcutta to Saint Teresa of Calcutta. She was our contemporary. Our knowledge of her life helps us to understand her humanity. She was a real person who needed a Savior just as we do. She did not set out as a believer to make

God doesn't call us to be successful; He calls us to be faithful.

134

herself a "headliner." On the contrary, she didn't have anything in mind but to follow where Christ led, even when that turned out to be the gutters of Calcutta. Her interest was in the good of others and the spread of the Gospel.

She kept her focus on Christ and obedience to His Word. Even the world's highest honors, including the Nobel Peace Prize, did not change her passion for society's castoffs.

Pope John Paul II said of Mother Teresa, "She had chosen to be not just the least but to be the servant of the least." She used her fame as a tool to do still more for these people she was called to serve. She was compelled to show her faith through her works.

Saints are not a thing of the past. They are walking in our midst today.

We can be like that. John Paul II also said, "True holiness does not mean a flight from the world; rather, it lies in the effort to incarnate the Gospel in everyday life, in the family, at school and at work, and in social and political involvement." That's the outward expression of inward change. That's the secret of sainthood.

Let's Talk

What's your mental picture of a "saint"? Do you know what influences helped to form that picture?
Would you call them positive or negative?

If you were to write a help-wanted ad for a saint, what qualities would you look for?

Among the people you know personally, who might you describe as having those qualities?
Do you know if there was a time in their lives when those qualities weren't as obvious?

The Bible provides detailed information about the sins of people God calls His own, like
King David and the Apostle Paul. Why would that information be important for us?

Is there someone in your circle of friends or family that people have declared hopeless?
What might prompt you to keep praying when there's no
reason to think the person is interested in change?

Many stories of transformation include incidents of success and failure.
What lessons about God's power and purpose do you think we can learn
from these stories and from our own successes and failures?

Let's Listen

Jonah 2   John 1   Romans 1:1–20

II Corinthians 5   Galatians 6

Let's Cook

LAND, AIR, AND SEA PAELLA

Preparing delicious foods is all about transformation. Raw ingredients that often seem incompatible are prepared according to the recipe and go from inedible to delicious! A good meal is a gentle show-and-tell reminder that it is entirely possible to be transformed and that God will apply heat if needed to make the process complete.

Remember: Different meats in the same dish often require different temperatures and different cooking times.

Land, Air, and Sea Paella

Serves: 8 | Prep Time: 20 Minutes | Cooking Time: 30 Minutes

1 tablespoon dried cilantro
½ teaspoon saffron
1 teaspoon paprika
1 teaspoon Old Bay Seasoning (or any dried seafood seasoning)
½ teaspoon salt
½ teaspoon pepper
2 boneless chicken breasts, cut into ½-inch cubes
2 Spanish chorizo sausages (or Italian sausages), cut into ¼-inch cubes
1 cup canned diced tomatoes
2 to 4 cups water (depending on how quickly rice cooks)

2 cups Corona or light beer (you can drink the rest)
1 8-ounce can chopped clams in juice
¼ cup extra-virgin olive oil
2 cups uncooked long-grain rice
4 garlic cloves, finely minced
1 yellow onion, diced
2 bay leaves
12 to 15 precooked frozen shrimp, thawed
3 to 4 tablespoons fresh flat-leaf parsley leaves
2 lemons, sliced into 6 to 8 slices, for garnish

[recipe continues on next page]

*All Saints' Day
reminds us that
God can make the
ordinary into
something
extraordinary—
He can change us
into saints!*

Combine cilantro, saffron, paprika, Old Bay, salt, and pepper in a small bowl. Place the chicken and sausage together in a medium bowl, toss with the dried spice mixture, and set aside.

In a separate bowl, combine the diced tomatoes, water, beer, and the can of chopped clams with juice. Set aside.

Heat 4 tablespoons of olive oil in a large pan (or paella pan) over medium high heat. Add the chicken and sausage mixture and cook for 7 to 10 minutes or until brown. The meat doesn't need to be completely cooked through at this point. Remove from the pan and set aside.

Add the rest of the olive oil to the pan and heat. Add rice and cook for about 30 seconds to 1 minute, or until the rice begins to take on some color. Add the garlic, onion, and bay leaves and sauté with the rice until the onions become translucent (approximately 1 to 2 minutes). Add the tomato-and-clam mixture to the pan and stir to mix all of the flavors together. Return the chicken and sausage to the pan and continue to cook for 15 to 20 minutes. Stir rice occasionally so that liquids simmer and the rice releases its starch. If liquids dry out too quickly before rice is soft, add 1 cup of hot water at a time and stir together.

Add precooked shrimp and allow it to warm for 1 to 2 minutes. Rice should be moist but not soupy. Rice at bottom of pan may begin to brown and caramelize, which is the desired texture. Before serving, add fresh parsley and stir together. Serve with lemon wedges as garnish.

CHAPTER 22

Courage and Convictions

Now as you excel in every respect, in faith, discourse, knowledge, all earnestness,

and in the love we have for you, may you excel in this gracious act also. . . .

For you know the gracious act of our Lord Jesus Christ, that for your sake

He became poor although He was rich, so that by His poverty you might become rich.

II CORINTHIANS 8:7—8

Imagine for a moment that you are Pietro Bernardone. You are a successful merchant and a leader in Assisi, your town in the beautiful region of Umbria, Italy. Your son Giovanni, who was nicknamed "Francesco" by his French mother, shows no interest in the family business, but until recently he has enjoyed the privileged lifestyle it provided. Lately, Francesco says he's had unusual dreams and even messages from God. After one of these messages, he took product out of your business inventory and sold it without your permission, along with the top-of-the-line transportation you had given him, and handed all the cash over to the local parish priest to fix up the church. The priest knew the money came from your resources, not your son's, and refused it. Your son responded by throwing the money on the ground.

When he learned you were angry, your son hid out for a month before you found him and brought him home. You grounded him, hoping he would come to his senses, but your wife let him out of the house, and he took refuge in a different church. Finally, to teach Francesco a lesson, you took him to court to cut off his inheritance, but Francesco declared that the court had no jurisdiction over him because God the Father is his true father. Francesco demonstrated the sincerity of his decision by removing all the clothing you provided for him and publicly renouncing all the human rights and comforts that would have been his. Francesco then went out into the hills beyond your hometown with no apparent plans for his future. The break has been total. You are at home without your son, wondering what would possess anyone, especially your own child, to walk away from the good life and welcome the prospect of poverty. You are sure he has traded his birthright for nothing of value.

From Pietro's point of view, his son was a failure. But with the benefit of historical perspective, we know better. Francesco was one of God's great successes. The story of his life has been told and retold from the thirteenth century to the twenty-first. Francesco's willingness to joyfully give up everything, do anything, and associate with anybody in order to show the love of Christ through his simple and pious life remains a model of godly living. Francesco's only goal was to use his life of poverty to help others

Saint Francis' story offers proof that God provides for every need when we trust Him.

find real riches in their faith. He rid himself of everything that hindered his ability to focus on the work of God. He wanted nothing for himself, but God gave him fame and honor beyond anything he could have achieved as the most renowned merchant. Francesco died in October 1226, and by July 1228 Pope Gregory IX had canonized him in recognition of all the good he had done for the least in God's kingdom. Francesco, the son Pietro could not get to conform, is the blessed Santo Francesco, Saint Francis of Assisi.

The man who wanted nothing for himself is now honored everywhere. His simple life sermon urging penance, brotherly love, and peace has challenged millions of believers and fueled the vocations of generations of priests and nuns who have been called into the orders he founded. They follow the humble example of Saint Francis by offering vows of poverty, chastity, and obedience to God. The good works of the Franciscans and the nuns of the Poor Clares, an order founded by St. Clare and inspired by Saint Francis, have been used by God on every continent.

Saint Francis' story offers so many lessons for families with teens. We see that God provides for every need when we trust Him. We have visible proof that the way to real happiness and contentment is not through the acquisition of things. And we're confronted with the fact that our children's future is not meant to be in our hands; their success might look like failure at first; the world might call them poor and inconsequential.

Saint Francis lived from 1182 until 1226. He is the patron saint of animals and is world famous, even to this day, for bringing hope to the weary.

By looking at the tug-of-war both Pietro Bernardone and Saint Clare's father, Favorino Scifi, Count of Sasso-Rosso, undertook in their attempts to keep their children from decisions they could not understand, we can see the futility of opposing God's plan. Loosen your grip, so God can hold your children close to Him.

Let's Talk

The first time Saint Francis was moved to help someone in need, the money he gave was his father's.

Why did this make his father so angry?

The first time Saint Francis had a dream, he saw sets of armor bearing crosses, and a voice said, "These are for your men." Saint Francis interpreted the dream to mean he would become a prince. Did he?

Church leaders opposed Saint Francis and Saint Clare when they insisted that they and the members of their orders own nothing, not just as individuals, but also as organizations.

What are the pros and cons of this position?

Have you ever heard someone say a task is "beneath his dignity"?

What does that mean? Can it be true?

If Saint Francis lived in your neighborhood, who would be on his list of people to care for?

What would he do for them? What might you do to follow his example?

If your parents absolutely opposed a decision you believed was directed by God, what would you do? How would you work toward a positive relationship?

Let's Listen

Deuteronomy 28:1–12   Psalm 27   Mark 12:28–34   II Corinthians 9

Let's Cook

What better way to honor the life of Saint Francis than to do good for someone else? Is there someone in your church who is confined to a wheelchair? Can you minister to that person by washing windows or scrubbing floors? Does he or

The juice of citrus fruits such as oranges, lemons, or limes can add a unique flavor to savory dishes like sausage or pork.

she need firewood for the months ahead or help with winterizing? On the day of your helpful visit, bring along a meal that is sure to have a lot of leftovers. That way, you can quietly leave some provisions behind and extend your ministry without causing embarrassment.

Orange and Rosemary Pork Skewers

Serves: 6 | Prep Time: 75 Minutes (Includes marinade) | Cooking Time: 30 Minutes

6 skewers (wooden or metal)
2 pounds pork roast cut into 1-inch cubes
  (measure to have 4 to 6 cubes per
  skewer)
1 teaspoon salt
½ teaspoon pepper
3 tablespoons olive oil
1 tablespoon orange zest
Juice of 1 orange
2 tablespoons fresh rosemary leaves, minced
  (or 1 tablespoon dried rosemary)
1 bag prewashed mixed field greens

Soak wooden skewers in water before cooking. Preheat oven to 375 degrees. Place pork cubes in a bowl. Combine salt, pepper, olive oil, orange zest, orange juice, and rosemary in a bowl. Pour over pork, mix, and marinate for about 1 hour.

Prepare skewers by adding 4 to 6 pieces of pork to each. Place skewers on a flat baking pan covered with aluminum foil. Pour extra sauce over the pork. Place in oven for 25 to 30 minutes, turning every 10 minutes. Serve hot skewers over the mixed field greens. Pour some of the hot marinade over greens to wilt and flavor them.

Tagliatelle ai Funghi Porcini

PORCINI MUSHROOM PASTA

Serves: 4 | Prep Time: 15 Minutes | Cooking Time: 20 Minutes

3 teaspoons salt

1-pound box tagliatelle pasta (a flat wide noodle—fettuccine is a good substitute)

½ cup olive oil

1 bag dried porcini mushrooms (or mixed dried mushrooms)

1 cup white wine

2 garlic cloves, minced

Pinch red pepper flakes

1 to 2 cups button mushrooms, chopped

1 cup hot starchy pasta water for the sauce

½ teaspoon black pepper

½ cup fresh grated Parmesan cheese plus extra for sprinkling

½ cup heavy whipping cream

2 tablespoons fresh parsley, chopped

Boil 2 quarts of water with 2 teaspoons of salt. Add pasta and 2 teaspoons of oil, stir, and continue to cook. Rehydrate the dried mushrooms: First rinse in cold water. Add the dried mushrooms to the white wine and put in the microwave for 1 minute, heating the wine and softening the mushrooms. Once cooled, remove the mushrooms from the wine (saving the wine) and chop the mushrooms finely. Set them aside.

In a separate pan, add remaining olive oil, garlic, and red pepper flakes and sauté over medium heat. Add the chopped mushrooms and the button mushrooms and sauté, being careful to avoid splashing the hot oil.

When pasta is al dente, reserve 1 cup of starchy water. Drain the rest of the water from the pasta. Return the pasta to the pot, add the hot olive oil–and-mushroom mixture. Turn heat to medium and continue to cook the pasta with mushroom oil. Add the mushroom-infused wine and the reserved 1 cup of hot starchy pasta water to the pasta and let cook for about 1 to 2 minutes more. Add remaining salt and the pepper.

Generally, this pasta does not have a lot of sauce but just enough flavored oil to cover each noodle. Add grated Parmesan cheese, heavy whipping cream, and fresh parsley. Let cook for another 1 to 2 minutes. Toss sauce and pasta together and serve with some extra grated Parmesan cheese.

CHAPTER 23

Goodness and Mercy

Give thanks to God, bless His name; good indeed is the LORD,

Whose love endures forever, whose faithfulness lasts through every age.

PSALM 100:4B—5

If Thanksgiving Day had an adjective, it would probably be "comfortable." There's something about the mood of the day that makes it easy to enjoy in any setting, with any group. Traditions may abound, but there are no "musts" that cannot be changed a bit from one year to the next, or changed back again by popular demand. It is a totally transportable celebration that has been observed onboard the space shuttle orbiting the earth and in military mess tents around the globe. It's for families, friends, even total strangers who are united for a few hours to share a meal and the blessings of a day that has a clear and simple mandate—say "thank you."

There are many diversions on Thanksgiving, and they seem to increase each year. Football games and parades have worked their way into the day, but they're fun to watch and have become a valued part of many gatherings. Some families tire of watching the television and hold their own annual touch-football classics in the backyard. These games take family bonding to a whole new level.

Another distraction at Thanksgiving comes via magazine editors and home décor experts intent on convincing hosts that color-coordinated place settings and table arrangements deserve more attention than the people gathered around the table. They want us to think that our china is able to do more for us than hold the cranberries.

So far, in spite of the pressures, most of us are refusing to trade the familiar for the fancy. Labor-intensive details like artfully arranging herb leaves to form a design under the skin of the turkey have just not caught on with most cooks! We know what matters most about Thanksgiving is being with the people for whom we are thankful. We appreciate the food, but when it comes to making our celebration memorable, the food does not compare with the company.

Family gatherings are not seamless productions. Your niece's recipe for lime gelatin salad may not improve with age. Your uncle's fondness for practical jokes may be as annoying as ever. Your cousin's date may go out of his way to make sure everyone knows his political views. But the flaws of today have a way of becoming the stories you'll share tomorrow as you recount your family history.

Thanksgiving Day reminds us that it's within the context of family that we learn how to appreciate and get along with people who don't share our opinions. In family we see that the process of aging can be both beautiful and difficult. Through family, we learn about bearing one another's burdens and sharing one another's joys; we find the strength to help with challenges we might have avoided if they faced a friend or neighbor. We learn to celebrate the fact that God picked this particular batch of less-than-perfect individuals to be our family. And when we see many of them gathered in one spot, joining hands to share a word of blessing over a meal that symbolizes all that God gives in response to our prayer for daily bread, we know what matters most to us and how we would start our list of that for which we are most thankful. Is it any wonder that the word "Eucharist"—Christ's sacred meal—literally means "thanksgiving"?

> *Thanksgiving is a holiday with a clear and simple mandate—say "thank you."*

Let's Talk

What is your best Thanksgiving Day memory?

What makes it so special to you?

If you were in charge of compiling this year's list of things for which
your family is thankful, what would make the top ten?

Prioritizing people and possessions in the right order is sometimes a struggle. Why do you think this is?

In his letter to the Philippians, the Apostle Paul acknowledged that the people of that church were
having a difficult time; he then said, "Rejoice in the Lord always. Again I shall say it, rejoice!"
How is it possible to be thankful or joyful when things do not seem to be going well?

Can you remember a circumstance that seemed awful when it happened but resulted in something good?

One of our national traditions is our attempt to ensure that everyone gets a Thanksgiving dinner.
How would you feel if you were serving a meal at a homeless shelter and knew that some of your
guests might be searching the dumpsters for their next meal?

Let's Listen

I Chronicles 16   Ezra 3   Psalm 100

II Corinthians 9   Philippians 4

Let's Cook

SAGE-MARINATED TURKEY BREAST
CREAMY MINT CRANBERRY SAUCE
ROASTED POTATOES AND FENNEL IN ANCHOVY BUTTER

Your Thanksgiving Day menu may be as much an heirloom as your family album. If you know your family won't be thankful for any change from their familiar green-bean casserole and bread stuffing,

> *Cooking parts of a turkey instead of a whole turkey at once is easier, saves time, and reduces leftovers.*

save these terrific recipes for another time when you want to celebrate the bounty God provides for our fellowship around the table.

Sage-Marinated Turkey Breast

Serves: 4 | Prep Time: 15 Minutes | Cooking Time: 40 Minutes

4 large boneless turkey breast cutlets
  (approximately 1 inch thick)
1 teaspoon salt
½ teaspoon pepper
1 cup Italian seasoned bread crumbs
4 tablespoons olive oil
1 tablespoon butter
1 tablespoon fresh sage leaves, finely
  chopped
1 tablespoon flour
½ cup white wine
½ cup water
Creamy Mint Cranberry Sauce (recipe
  follows)

Preheat oven to 375 degrees. Season turkey breasts on both sides with salt and pepper and cover with bread crumbs. In a frying pan, heat olive oil over high heat. Add the breasts and sear for 2 minutes on each side. Remove and set aside.

In the same pan, turn heat to medium and add butter, chopped sage, and flour to create a roux. Slowly add white wine and water, whisking to break up lumps. Let simmer and thicken. Pour sauce over the turkey and cover with foil. Bake in oven for approximately 35 to 40 minutes.

Divide the turkey breasts among four dinner plates. Ladle 2 to 3 tablespoons of the cranberry sauce over each serving of turkey.

Creamy Mint Cranberry Sauce

Serves: 4 | Prep Time: 5 Minutes | Cooking Time: 15 Minutes

2 tablespoons butter
1 teaspoon fresh mint, finely chopped
1 tablespoon sugar
¼ teaspoon salt
1 tablespoon flour
1 cup heavy whipping cream
8 ounces canned cranberry dressing
¼ cup dried cranberries

Melt butter in a saucepan over medium heat. Add the mint, sugar, salt, and flour to thicken the butter and create a loose paste. Slowly add the heavy whipping cream, whisking to prevent lumps. Add canned cranberry dressing, breaking it up to create a creamy pink sauce. Add dried cranberries and let come to a soft boil. Serve.

Roasted Potatoes and Fennel in Anchovy Butter

Serves: 4 | Prep Time: 15 Minutes | Cooking Time: 30 Minutes

2 anchovy fillets, minced
4 to 5 tablespoons salted butter
2 garlic cloves, minced
4 medium-sized red potatoes, cut in halves
    (or ¼-inch cubes)
4 fennel bulbs, cleaned and cut into ½-inch
    sections, stems and leaves removed
1 teaspoon salt
½ tablespoon black pepper
2 teaspoons parsley, fresh chopped

Preheat oven to 375 degrees. In a saucepan, sauté minced anchovies, butter, and garlic over medium heat. In a baking dish, add potatoes and fennel. (The fennel will break up like an onion, so there is no need to be exact with the ½-inch pieces.)

Once the anchovy-and-butter mixture is melted, pour it over the potato-and-fennel mixture. Season with salt and pepper. Place in oven. After 20 to 25 minutes, turn the oven to broil for about 5 minutes or until edges begin to brown. Sprinkle parsley as garnish before serving.

CHAPTER 24

'Tis the Season

A voice cries out in the desert: Prepare the way of the LORD! Make straight in the

wasteland a highway for our God! Every valley shall be filled in, every mountain

and hill shall be made low; the rugged land shall be made a plain, the rough

country, a broad valley. Then the glory of the LORD shall be revealed,

and all mankind shall see it together.

ISAIAH 40:3—5

Did you know there's a vaccine that prevents the hard-to-define disappointment and emptiness so many people feel when the Christmas tree comes down? It's found in Advent.

Advent is a time of spiritual preparation and anticipation. It provides a solid framework families can use to protect Christmas from being drained of its true meaning and spiritual blessings. Observing Advent at home and at church creates family time in the weeks before Christmas. When you pause to celebrate Advent, you focus on God's promises about the coming of Christ and anticipate the family Christmas traditions that mean the most to you.

Looking at the Old Testament prophecies and the richness of their detail, we see how intimately God is involved in the planning of Christ's incarnation. Our holiday preparation is truly holy-day preparation, which should be marked by a wise investment of our time and resources rather than a waste of them.

Celebrating Advent at church and at home in our devotions, or by using a traditional Advent wreath or calendar to mark each day until Christmas, helps strengthen our ability to resist the clutter. When we appreciate the beauty of the real story of Christmas, we are able to put everything else in perspective.

The world pulls hard on us, attempting to divert our attention, our energy, and our budget, enticing us to join the frenzy called the holiday season. It offers a distorted shell of the real holiday, emptied of the very reason for the existence of Christmas. On the outside, it's all glitter and excitement; at its core, it's empty and melancholy. Advent is our life raft on a

Advent provides a solid framework families can use to protect Christmas from being drained of its true meaning.

sea of sale circulars, invitations, skating elves, and inflatable snowmen.

Advent shows us that giving and receiving gifts is not an end in itself, but a representation of God's unmatchable gift to us. Advent reveals the importance of the genealogy recorded in the first chapter of the New Testament. Advent introduces the participants in the original nativity pageant. Advent tells us why the Magi were on their search; why Herod was worried; why Jesus had to be born in Bethlehem; and why we must not go along with the crowd, secularizing an event that is quintessentially sacred.

Week by week, we can make our homes and events a refuge for those who want to experience the true spirit of the season. We can gently point the way to a celebration that will not leave a bad aftertaste. We can create an environment where holiday memories will be of time spent with friends and loved ones. We can orient our sons and daughters to find the enjoyment in giving, especially in giving of their time and abilities. The genuine appreciation on the face of a child receiving his first toy reminds us of how many gifts we have taken for granted. By making the most of Advent, we can ensure that the Christmas spirit will linger in our homes long into the new year. Ultimately, Advent is a time to prepare for the greatest gift imaginable. The gift is not a what, but a who!

Advent begins four Sundays before Christmas. It's a time of patience, waiting, and prayer! Prepare well for Christmas by not rushing Advent.

Let's Talk

What is your favorite family tradition between Thanksgiving and Christmas? What makes it special?

You've grown up being told it is "more blessed to give than to receive." How can that be true?

If your family decided to not spend money on gifts for each other and donate that money instead, what are some gift ideas that don't cost anything? Where would you want the donation to go?

Have you ever thought about Jesus' human ancestors? Why do you think their names are in the Bible? Does anybody in your extended family keep track of your family tree? Have you ever been surprised by something you've learned about your heritage?

If you could change one thing about the holiday season, what would it be?

How does knowing that specific prophesies were fulfilled in Christ's birth affect your interest in the prophesies of His return?

Let's Listen

Genesis 3:15   Genesis 22   Psalm 72   Isaiah 7

Micah 5:2   Matthew 1   Luke 1

Let's Cook

MEATBALLS IN CREAMY VODKA SAUCE

Give your family the gift of time together this season. Simple meals that take advantage of the Crock-Pot or the microwave reduce prep time so you can have more time around the table, catching up with one another. Save some money and take advantage of your family's love of good food by creating custom gifts of cookies, jams, baked goods, soup mixes, pasta dinner baskets, or collections of your favorite recipes. Gifts like these are fun to make and wonderful to receive.

Meatballs in Creamy Vodka Sauce

Serves: 6 | Prep Time: 20 Minutes | Cooking Time: 20 Minutes

MEATBALLS
2 pounds ground beef
1 onion, finely chopped
½ teaspoon garlic powder
½ teaspoon salt and pepper
2 eggs
¼ cup Italian bread crumbs
2 tablespoons soy sauce
1 cup all-purpose flour
4 tablespoons olive oil

CREAMY VODKA SAUCE
1 tablespoon olive oil
2 garlic cloves, minced
1 medium-sized white onion, minced
2 tablespoons fresh parsley, chopped
32 ounces tomato sauce
1 6-ounce can tomato paste
1 cup heavy whipping cream
½ teaspoon salt
¼ teaspoon black pepper
3 pinches red pepper flakes
½ cup vodka

To make the meatballs, use your hands to combine ground beef, onion, garlic powder, salt, pepper, eggs, bread crumbs, and soy sauce in a bowl. When thoroughly mixed, shape into meatballs about the size of golf balls. Roll them in flour and shake off excess.

Heat olive oil over medium heat in a skillet and add meatballs. Cook until brown on all sides. Set aside to cool. (After cooling, you can freeze the meatballs for later use.)

To prepare the vodka sauce, heat olive oil in a large pot or pan over medium heat. Sauté garlic, onion, and parsley until onion becomes translucent, approximately 2 to 3 minutes. Add tomato sauce, tomato paste, and heavy whipping cream. Stir well. Add salt, black pepper, red pepper flakes, and finally the vodka. Continue to stir and let simmer for about 2 to 3 minutes or until the smell of alcohol is not as strong.

Add meatballs—enough to be covered by the sauce. Cook with the lid slightly off the pot in order to release some steam. Let simmer for at least 10 minutes, letting the sauce take in the flavors of the meatballs.

To Serve as Subs
Preheat oven to 375 degrees. Toast regular sub rolls in the oven for 3 to 5 minutes. Brush buns with olive oil and add 3 to 4 meatballs per bun. Top with fresh mozzarella cheese and heat in oven for another 2 minutes to melt the cheese.

To Serve as Appetizers
Place meatballs in a flat dish with a small bowl of vodka sauce for dipping. Place toothpicks next to this tray, as well as some pita bread wedges or slices of French baguette.

Ask your children to help in the kitchen by cooking or cleaning up after a party. It's a gift I'm sure all parents would enjoy!

CHAPTER 25

Joy, Joy, Joy

SUGGESTED FOR THE CHRISTMAS SEASON

For God so loved the world that he gave his only Son, so that everyone who believes in

him might not perish but might have eternal life. For God did not send His Son into

the world to condemn the world, but that the world might be saved through Him.

JOHN 3:16—17

Do your holiday decorations include a crèche? Can you picture that incredible moment? God loves us so much that He willingly sent Jesus, His only Son, to be one of us, to live among us, and die for us so that we could live with Him forever. It is a gift of such enormity that there are not words to describe it.

To help us grasp the wonder of this event that changed the course of human history, the Apostle John begins his Gospel in this way: "In the beginning was the Word, and the Word was with God, and the Word was God. He was in the beginning with God. All things came to be through Him, and without Him nothing came to be. What came to be through Him was life, and this life was the light of the human race. . . . And the Word became flesh and made His dwelling among us, and we saw His glory, the glory as of the Father's only Son, full of grace and truth." The Light of the World was born into the humblest of circumstances in a place called Bethlehem. He made His dwelling with us.

Consider that as you celebrate Christ's birth. The Light of the human race, God the Son, made

Himself at home with us. That is the reason for Christmas. Nothing else we associate with the holiday comes close to this. It doesn't matter if there is a single present under the tree—or even if there is a tree at all. It doesn't matter if the house is packed full of kids, or if circumstances keep you from gathering together. Nothing about your personal situation, not the sadness of separation, not illness or death, not poverty, nothing can cast a shadow on the celebration of the birth of our Savior and King.

> *When Christ is the center of the celebration, everything else about this holy day and the season surrounding it falls into its proper place.*

When Christ is the center of the celebration, everything else about this holy day and the season surrounding it falls into its proper place. The giving and receiving of gifts becomes what it should be, symbolic of the ultimate Gift and not an end in itself. The popular stories about Santa Claus, the Grinch, Rudolph, elves, and all the fictional characters who have crept into the season are moved from center stage to their subsidiary place with the tinsel and twinkling lights. From there, parents can choose to ignore these stories or include them without letting fiction supplant truth. Parents are free to explain to their children from the very beginning that the Christmas presents they receive are given by people who love them, and that they represent God's unconditional love for all of His children.

This freedom to celebrate the heart of the holiday releases your family from the crazed competitions that measure winners and losers by the height of the tree, the wattage of the lawn display, the size of the stack of packages, and the balance due on the credit cards. All of that is replaced with the simple pleasures of family time and family traditions, new and old, which put the emphasis on giving instead of getting.

Give your kids the gift of simple pleasures like a cookie-making party with their friends (be sure to make lots of extras for guests to take home for their parents). Organize the neighbors for an evening of caroling, followed by hot cocoa at your place. Decorate a tree for the birds who visit your yard in winter. Ask your local Christmas bureau for the name of a family in need. Buy gifts for each of them (and fewer for each other). Open your home to someone who would otherwise spend Christmas alone. Sometime during the Christmas season, read the Christmas story together. End it with a quiet moment that brings you back to the manger to sing with the angels and bow with the Magi. O come let us adore Him!

Christ has come!
Merry Christmas!
Maligayan Pasko!
Feliz Navidad!
Joyeux Noël!
Buone Feste Natalizie!
Kala Christouyenna!
Sung Tan Chuk Ha!
Joy to the World!

Let's Talk

When you were younger, what part in the nativity pageant did you most want to have? What was its appeal? Have you ever wondered what it would have been like to be at the actual nativity?

What is your favorite Christmas memory? Does Christmas sometimes seem less fun as you get older? Have you thought about why or how it could be more fun again?

Some people go into a lot of debt to buy Christmas presents. Why would they do that? What are some alternatives?

How do you feel when you and your friends compare Christmas presents? Do you think that conversations like that are harder for some of your friends than others?

What's the oddest Christmas present you ever got? What's the most unique gift you ever gave? Why is giving and receiving gifts part of Christmas, not some other holiday?

Christmas makes some people depressed. How can you or your family encourage people who are having a hard time coping while others are celebrating?

Let's Listen

Isaiah 9:1–7   Matthew 2   Luke 2

John 1   Hebrews 1

Let's Cook

SAUSAGE-AND-SAGE-STUFFED CORNISH GAME HENS WITH CREAMY BAKED BREAD AND ROOT VEGETABLE SIDE STUFFING

Have you ever considered the many moments we know about in Jesus' life that are connected to meals? He blessed the loaves and fishes and fed the multitude; He hosted the Passover meal and established the sacrament of Holy Communion; after His resurrection, He greeted His disciples with breakfast when they returned from fishing in the Sea of Galilee. At that meal, our Savior said to the Apostle Peter, "Feed my sheep." Over and over He invites us to His table to receive the bread of life. This Christmas, remember to praise the Father for the gift of Christ and make Him the honored guest at your table.

Sausage-and-Sage-Stuffed Cornish Game Hens

Serves: 6 | Prep Time: 15 Minutes | Cooking Time: 80 Minutes

FILLING
2 Italian sausages cooked according to instructions and cooled and finely chopped into small pieces
5 fresh sage leaves
2 cups bread crumbs
2 tablespoons mayonnaise
1 teaspoon orange zest

PREPARING CORNISH GAME HENS
6 Cornish game hens
3 tablespoons extra-virgin olive oil
2 teaspoons salt
1 teaspoon pepper
2 teaspoons paprika
1 orange, cut into 6 wedges

CREAMY BAKED BREAD AND ROOT VEGETABLE SIDE STUFFING
8 slices white bread, cut or "ripped" into ¼-inch squares
2 stalks celery, cut into ¼-inch pieces
2 carrots, cut into ¼-inch pieces
1 apple, cut into ¼-inch pieces
¾ cup dried cranberries
1 green pepper, cut into ¼-inch pieces
1 onion, cut into ¼-inch pieces
1 cup heavy whipping cream (or milk)
1 cup white wine
1 cup chicken broth
1 teaspoon salt
1 teaspoon black pepper
2 tablespoons melted butter

BASTING SAUCE
2 tablespoons butter
1 cup chicken stock or broth

[recipe continues on next page]

Combine all of the filling ingredients together, making a paste-like stuffing. Set aside in order to prepare the game hens.

Wash and clean game hens at room temperature. Discard innards or freeze for future recipes. Dry hens with a paper towel. Drizzle olive oil to lightly coat the exterior of each hen. Salt and pepper both inside and outside of each hen. Sprinkle paprika over hens and rub with hands to evenly distribute seasoning. Insert one orange wedge and one large spoonful of the stuffing to fill cavity. Set aside and prepare side stuffing.

To prepare the side stuffing, spray bottom and sides of a large baking dish with nonstick spray. Incorporate all of the side stuffing ingredients together and mix thoroughly.

Place each hen on top of a baker's rack over top of the stuffing, leaving 1 to 2 inches between each hen. The juices of the hens will continue to drip onto the stuffing.

Cover the whole dish with aluminum foil and place in a 400-degree oven. After 50 minutes, drop the oven temperature to 375 degrees. Remove the foil and continue to cook for another 30 minutes. Baste with basting sauce every 10 to 15 minutes.

To baste: Use a saucepan to melt 2 tablespoons of butter with 1 cup of chicken stock or broth. Let this come to a slight simmer and use a brush to baste the hens.

Cook hens according to instructions per weight or until you see the juices run clean when pierced with a fork. The juices from the hens and the basting liquid will continue to drip onto the bread stuffing and cook all of the ingredients so the flavors run together.

After hens are cooked, remove and let rest for about 10 to 15 minutes. Mix stuffing and let cook in oven for another 10 to 15 minutes.

CHAPTER 26

A Day in the Life of Families

TACKLING THE THROWDOWNS IN OUR LIVES

Let us not grow tired of doing good, for in due time we shall reap our harvest, if we do not give up.

GALATIANS 6:9

Some rather profound things are said at the end of every episode of the Food Network Show *Throwdown with Bobby Flay*. If you recall, the crowd gathers around the superstar chef and his competitor. The camera focuses on Bobby Flay, who says, "So to all you awesome cooks out there, keep doing what you're doing, but ask yourself this . . ." Then his competitor says, "Are you ready for a throwdown?" The crowd erupts with cheers, and with that the show is over. But life goes on.

What's so profound is that the question touches the hearts of all people, no matter what religion, age, gender, or economic status. The question isn't just about a cooking competition either. It's about life! Are we ready? In other words, life can be tough. Can we handle it? This is a question that families ask every day. And if you're a family that has experienced some crisis, you know the

only way to get through another day is with God's grace.

I'd like to dedicate this chapter to all of those awesome families out there who may need the encouragement to "keep doing what you're doing!" Keep trying. Keep plugging along. It's the only way to live. The alternative is to give up. And that's not an option for those who live in reality! The only real choice is to choose life and persevere!

Perseverance is a unique word. It is packed with meaning. In it are the words *per*, meaning "through," and *severe*. Need I say more? Implied in this word, however, are the virtues of faith, hope, and love. The only way we get through anything "severe" is if we truly know and believe from the depth of our being that we can make it with God's help, if we have hope that we are not alone in our struggles, and if we love something or someone enough that we will endure even the most challenging situations.

The idea behind Grace Before Meals actually began as a result of some challenges: the severe challenge of September 11 and the ongoing challenge to persevere in raising a child with special needs.

Let me explain.

September 11, 2001, is a date that I hope this world holds in sacred memory. I was supposed to go to France with two priest friends a few days later, but all flights were canceled for obvious security reasons. Instead of going on this pilgrimage, we stayed in our parishes to offer pastoral care for a weekend of masses packed with all types of people— some who come irregularly, many who'd never graced the doors of the church in their lives. Everyone seemed to "need" church after the tragedies turned our world upside down. It was as if people were coming "home" looking for some comfort, meaning, and just to spend time with other people who believed in something better and hopeful.

People packed the church simply because they wanted to be together, and above all, to be with God. Isn't that what church provides? It's a place to be together, with God and with other believers, around a sacred meal that comforts our hurting bodies, our confused minds, and our troubled souls.

After a tough weekend of pastoral duties, my friends and I used the rest of our scheduled pilgrimage time and went to a simple retreat house near the ocean. We also needed time for prayer, reflection, and brotherhood. After all, priests are human, too. To save us time and to develop our fraternity, we cooked most of our meals. Of course, I did most of the cooking and my friends didn't seem to mind that one bit. While cooking, one priest came into the kitchen to watch me prep the meal, which I believe was lobster—talk about comfort food! He commented about how he enjoyed watching me cook, and that he thought that such a concept—a priest cooking show— would be fun. He explored the idea out loud and became rather excited about the possibilities of a show that combined food, faith, family, and fun. It was exactly what the world needed, especially during our troubled period of history. It was a show, or actually a movement, that would bring God back to the dinner table. Somehow, I would be the cook and host of these meals.

I thought it was one of the silliest ideas I'd ever heard. The idea of the show was understandable and actually quite worthy. But for *me* to be the host seemed absolutely silly. Still, my other priest friend chimed in in agreement, and soon I felt like I needed to take it seriously. But I didn't. Instead, I jokingly agreed and said, "We should call it *Grace Before Meals*!" The idea spread among some of the other priests, and soon they began asking me questions about the show. They also agreed that positive TV shows are very much needed, and anything to help families grow stronger together is worth every priest's effort.

Looking back, I marvel about how such a tragedy like September 11 can initiate the creative aspect of our compassion to the point of suggesting a priest cooking show. God certainly works in marvelous ways, but could He work in *this* way? Sometimes I wondered if the idea was a "gimmick" that might lead me to pride, or a "calling" that would require my humble obedience.

I had to leave these questions to God's initiative, because any impression that I was somehow "pushing" the show unsettled my spirit and left me feeling rather unpriestly. In due time, God would slowly reveal and lay out His plan. In fact, even though I wasn't really thinking about it too seriously after our post-9/11 retreat, God responded to some of my questions two years later.

Fast forward to Lent, 2003. I was transferred to another parish assignment in Westminster, Maryland. I was in the sacristy after Mass with another priest when a man came in just to chat a few moments with us. This is very typical, and I thought nothing of it. He introduced himself as Tim Watkins. He explained that he felt the need to come to church on a daily basis, not just as a Lenten discipline, but also because he somehow was seeking inner strength to help him to be a good husband and father. He had a wonderful wife and three children. He felt blessed, even though he experienced challenges at times because his youngest child, Brian, had autism.

If you are parents of a child with special needs, you know how it can bring you to your knees in prayer. Dealing with such difficult and severe personal situations takes God's grace and strength to care for such special family members. The emptiness that comes from the absence of grace is unfortunately filled with fear and the temptation to take what may seem practical measures and make deadly choices, such as abandonment. Tim and his wife knew that care for this special child required grace above all else. For Tim, abandonment wasn't an issue. He was simply seeking more of God's grace to be the husband and dad he was called to be. That's why he came to church that day.

Yet our conversation wasn't even *that* deep. In fact, it was just a general and almost generic introduction. In an effort to keep the conversation going, the question came up, "Tim, what do you do for a living?" Innocently, he explained that he owned a creative services and production company that produced shows and commercials for the cable industry. Almost instantly, the other priest in the room, who knew about my *Grace Before Meals* idea/joke, blurted out, "Well have I got an idea for you!" In what I characterize as an awkward moment, Tim listened as the other priest explained *Grace Before Meals*—a priest cooking show that can help strengthen family relationships around the dinner table!

It was uncomfortable to hear about all of this, because I still didn't think that anything would come of it. Little did I know that God's grace was at work.

While none of us were ready for such an idea to take off, there was an eventual and mutual agreement that this concept needed to be fleshed out—incarnate! Good ideas are not meant to remain in the realm of theory. Like God, the Word becomes flesh to dwell among us, because Jesus Christ is not just a "good idea" for a religion. He is real—in the flesh and blood! Similarly, what I originally thought was a reasonably "good idea" eventually became a website, a book, a Web series, and now an international movement that has left me wondering how marvelous is God's wisdom. *Grace Before Meals* is no longer a concept. It is real and has touched tens of thousands of lives.

On deeper reflection, I realize how this movement started with a challenge to persevere: September 11 and a father's prayer for grace to help him raise his children—in particular his son with special needs.

Within a day in the life of a typical family, we find that nothing is "typical." Sure, there are those days when nothing seems too problematic, days that perhaps are even boring. But there are also those days when families experience great tragedies and struggles. What gets a family through the struggles—national tragedies, special needs children, accidents, job loss, unplanned pregnancies, health concerns, break-ups, peer rejections, addictions, you name it—isn't a government official, a bailout, a drink, a relationship, or winning the lottery. It's perseverance through a life lived with faith, hope, and love.

These are not "concepts" that remain in the realm of theory. These are realities that can take on flesh if we're willing to allow grace to touch our lives and our meals! These words are more than just happy thoughts. These are virtues that give people interior strength to persevere. Grace is real. I've seen it for myself at dinner tables across this country.

In a day in the life of a family, how often does the family come together—as a "domestic church"—to give each other support, encouragement, and positive company? After September 11, it seemed the world needed the church family to embrace its hurting members. After taking stock of his own life, it seemed that Tim also needed the communion of saints to help his own family, especially when he realized that his autistic son is his guardian angel that was sent by God to help his family become saints, too.

In the day of the life of the family, does the Church play a role? The Church exists as a family to help each other in good times and bad, sickness and health, whether you're rich or poor. In fact, the Church exists as a promise of God's love for humanity! God established the Church to help us get from real life to eternal life. The presence of the Church is as enduring as the promise made between man and woman on their wedding day.

If a family doesn't gather regularly around a meal, then how does the "idea" of "a close-knit family" get fleshed out? If families don't share a moment together around the comfort of their own table, to share the blessings of the food and each other, and to thank God for these blessings, then grace withers away, and the idea of "family life" remains only an idea. Will the hope of a stronger family remain just a theory or a concept? Sound theology and the Church's solemn feast days remind us that persevering faith, abiding hope, and everlasting love are supposed to "come to life" and "take on flesh" in each of us. This extends to the family when they are willing to persevere—not just in the good times, but also in bad times, and especially during the boring, regular, mundane times, which just so happen to be real life.

The reason why people of faith can call particular challenges and tragedies "blessings in disguise" is because these decisive moments make us

remember the presence of God working in our lives to bring out the best in us, even when the challenges feel like they are bringing out the worst in us. People who lived until September 12, 2001, realized that each day is a gift, each person is worth paying attention to, and every challenge is supposed to make us stronger. For families who have special needs children, they realize the blessings of their own health as a gift—not for themselves—but to be shared with others who are not as physically or mentally healthy. The example of family as caregivers for God's special ones on this earth is a sign of God's promise: His love takes on flesh, and His love endures forever!

Remember, God's love is not a theory, idea, or concept. The love is a reality that can truly take on flesh when we are willing to let grace touch our lives.

This chapter, this book, the show, and the entire movement called Grace Before Meals is dedicated to all of God's awesome families! Keep doing what you're doing. But ask yourself this: Are you ready for a throwdown? Believe me, in the daily lives of families, challenges will come. But *Grace Before Meals* is here to help you persevere and to strengthen your family, one dinner at a time!

> *Remember, God's love is not a theory, idea, or concept. The love is a reality that can truly take on flesh when we are willing to let grace touch our lives.*

Let's Talk

Do you remember what you were doing on September 11, 2001?

How did you and your family deal with this tragic day?

Do your children who weren't yet born know about this day? When and how will you tell them?

Do you have any special prayers or Bible verses that help you when you are challenged or face difficulties?

Have you ever met a family with children who have special needs?

What are some positive things that you have learned in your experience or observation of them?

Have you ever had to give advice and encouragement to someone facing a big problem?

What would you tell that person?

Have you ever thought of the family as a "domestic church"?

What does that mean for you, your family, and your relationship to the Church?

Has there ever been a time when you went to a church or a sacred shrine all alone,

just to ask for special prayers? What was it like to be there alone?

Did you feel "lonely," or were you able to detect God's presence at that moment?

How have the virtues of faith, hope, and love become incarnate—taken on flesh—in your family life?

Let's Listen

Psalm 42:6   1 Peter 1:3   Deuteronomy 31:6   Matthew 11: 28–30

Let's Cook

MOM'S CHICKEN ADOBO WITH LEMONGRASS-INFUSED COCONUT CURRY SAUCE MY VERSION OF MOM'S PANCIT

God's grace is rarely bold, like a habanero pepper or a bite into a clove of garlic. His grace is subtle, like a hint of sage or pinch of parsley, and it finds us in those moments when we least expect it, but truly need it the most. When tasting a new dish or an old favorite, or simply going about your everyday life, seek out those subtle flavors and those little moments of God's grace. The taste is exquisite.

Mom's Chicken Adobo with Lemongrass-Infused Coconut Curry Sauce

Serves 4 to 6 | Cooking Time: 15 Minutes | Prep Time: 30 Minutes

2 tablespoons vegetable oil
2 garlic cloves, minced
6 to 8 pieces of chicken (you can select any pieces), bone in and with skin (removing the skin is optional, but risks the chicken getting dry)
1 tablespoon salt
2 tablespoons Chinese five-spice powder (or 1 packet of adobo mixture)
2 whole bay leaves
1 large white onion, quartered
1 cup soy sauce
½ cup apple cider vinegar
1 teaspoon whole black peppercorns
6-inch branch lemongrass
1 tablespoon dry curry powder
1 cup coconut milk

Heat oil in a large pot, and sauté garlic over medium heat. Season chicken with salt and five-spice powder. Add chicken to the pot and cook until lightly browned on at least two sides of each piece, about 2 minutes on each side. Add the bay leaves, onion, soy sauce, vinegar, and black peppercorns. Mix together. Keep pot covered, stirring occasionally, and cook for about 15 minutes. Add lemongrass, curry powder, and coconut milk and mix. Reduce heat to simmer for another 10 to 15 minutes, uncovered, stirring occasionally. Remove lemongrass and bay leaves before serving with hot sticky rice.

My Version of Mom's Pancit

A FILIPINO VEGETABLE AND CHICKEN NOODLE DISH—
ADAPTED FOR AMERICANIZED INGREDIENTS

Serves 4 to 6 | Cooking Time: 15 Minutes | Prep Time: 25 Minutes

1 pound rice noodles (gluten-free) or
    Italian vermicelli, cooked al dente (see
    instructions on package)
1 tablespoon peanut oil
1 tablespoon vegetable oil
2 garlic cloves, finely minced
1 cup shredded carrots
1 cup finely shredded cabbage
½ cup onion, sliced into thin half moons
2 medium-sized celery stalks, thinly shredded
    (about 1 cup)
1 pound chicken thighs, deboned, skinned,
    and thinly sliced
½ teaspoon salt
½ teaspoon black pepper
1 tablespoon oyster sauce (special ingredient
    found in international section of grocery,
    or Asian market)
¼ cup soy sauce
¼ cup water
½ to 1 tablespoon hot chili sauce, *sriracha*
    (optional)
Reserved leaves from the celery stalk,
    minced

Cook the noodles according to instructions, drain, and set aside.

Heat peanut oil and vegetable oil in a wok or large nonstick pan. Sauté garlic, carrots, cabbage, onion, and shredded celery for 1 minute. Add chicken meat, salt, and pepper, and cook for 3 to 4 minutes, stirring to incorporate all the flavors until chicken is fully cooked. Add oyster sauce, soy sauce, water, and hot chili sauce (if using), and cook until water evaporates and sauce begins to thicken.

Remove from heat and add noodles, mixing to incorporate all of the flavors. Top off with minced celery leaves.

Cooking Tip
Partially frozen chicken thighs are easier to cut than thawed ones

Prayers

As you gather around the table to share a meal, why not also share a moment of thanks and prayer? Here are a few examples of some traditional blessings and "freestyle" prayers, but feel free to create your own prayers as well. They don't need to be long or complicated – just a few simple heartfelt words can help your family experience true grace and grow closer together.

Bless, O Christ God,
the food and drink of Your
servants,
for You are holy,
now and always and ever,
and unto the ages of ages.
Amen.

Bless us O Lord,
and these, Thy gifts,
which we are about to receive,
through Christ our Lord.
Amen.

God is great,
God is good,
Let us praise God
for this table
and food.

We give You thanks O Lord,
for these and all Thy gifts,
which we have received
through Christ our Lord.
And, may the souls of the
faithful departed,
through the Mercy of God,
rest in peace.
Amen.

The eyes of all look to You,
O Lord.
You give them their food
in due season.
You open Your hand
and fill every living thing with
Your blessing.
Sanctify us, we beseech You,
through word and prayer;
and give Your blessing
to these gifts
which of Your bounty we are
about to receive,
through Christ our Lord.
Amen.

Blessing Prayer in Latin:
Oremus. Bendic, Domine,
nos et haec tua dona,
quae de tua largitate sumus
sumpturi.
Per Christum Dominum
nostrum.
Amen.

Blessing After Meal in Latin:
Agimus tibi gratias,
omnipotens Deus,
pro universis beneficiis tuis,
qui visis et regnas in saecula
saeculorum.
Amen.

Grant Your blessings
to this food,
that it may nourish us
and strengthen us
to do Your will
and to serve those
who go without.

Loving Father, we thank you
for the family gathered
around the table,
the friends who extend
Your goodness,
the food which nourishes
our bodies,
and the Faith that
strengthens our souls.
Keep us ever mindful of
these blessings,
and may this food inspire us
to bring these blessings to those
who go without family, friends,
food, and faith.
We ask all of this
through Christ our Lord.
Amen.

173

Metric Conversion Chart

Liquids

U.S.		Imperial		Metric	
1	teaspoon	⅙	fluid ounce	5	milliliters
1	tablespoon	½	fluid ounce	15	milliliters
⅛	cup	1	fluid ounce	30	milliliters
¼	cup	2	fluid ounces	60	milliliters
½	cup	4	fluid ounces	120	milliliters
¾	cup	6	fluid ounces	180	milliliters
1	cup	8	fluid ounces	240	milliliters
1	pint (2 cups)	16	fluid ounces	470	milliliters
1	quart (4 cups)	32	fluid ounces	950	milliliters
1	gallon (4 quarts)	128	fluid ounces	3.8	liters

Oven Temperatures

Type of Heat	°Fahrenheit	°Celcius
Very Low	225	107
	250	121
Low	275	135
	300	148
Moderate	325	162
	350	176
Moderately High	375	190
	400	204
High	425	218
	450	232
Very High	475	246

Recipe Index